To Tara & Wa

Please don't recycle!

Mike Nevins
8/09

A TALE OF TWO "VILLAGES":
VINELAND AND SKILLMAN, NJ

The unknown story of New Jersey's major role in promoting eugenics theory which indirectly led to sterilization of more than 65,000 Americans and to mass murder in Nazi Germany.

MICHAEL NEVINS

iUniverse, Inc.
New York   Bloomington

iUniverse books may be ordered through booksellers or by contacting:

iUniverse
1663 Liberty Drive
Bloomington, IN 47403
www.iuniverse.com
1-800-Authors (1-800-288-4677)

ISBN: 978-1-4401-4261-1 (sc)
ISBN: 978-1-4401-4262-8 (ebook)

Printed in the United States of America

iUniverse rev. date: 5/28/2009

To Rachel, Talya, David, Leora, Sam, Julia, and Ava

Contents

Preface

In 2003, investigative journalist Edwin Black published *War Against The Weak: Eugenics and America's Campaign to Create a Master Race.* The book's main thesis was that the eugenics movement, which had a wide following in our country early in the last century, sought to terminate the nation's most vulnerable and helpless citizens, the mentally handicapped, by selective breeding in the name of human improvement. The author described how "a phalanx of elite shock troops" sallied forth to influence public opinion, shrouding their racist beliefs under the protective canopy of science. In tandem, they would hunt, identify, label and take control of those deemed unfit to populate the earth.[1]

In his well-researched book, Mr. Black devoted much attention to psychiatrist Dr. Edwin Katzen-Ellenbogen, who had emigrated from Germany to the United States in 1905, married an American woman, became a naturalized citizen and converted from Judaism to her Christian religion. Being a long-time student of Jewish medical history, I was intrigued by this individual who reportedly worked for several years in a mental hospital in Massachusetts, sometimes lectured on abnormal psychology at Harvard Medical School, and also was an enthusiastic eugenicist. In 1911 Dr. Katzen-Ellenbogen moved to New Jersey, where he worked for little more than a year before leaving his wife and child and returning to Europe. He dropped out of public view for two decades, then reemerged in 1947 at a war crimes trial that was conducted at Dachau, the former German concentration camp, by the U.S. Army. Because of his Jewish heritage, Katzen-Ellenbogen had been arrested by the Gestapo, was sent to Buchenwald and, while imprisoned there, had collaborated with the Nazis. At the Dachau trial the doctor was asked to bear witness against his former captors, but as more facts emerged the tables turned, and Katzen-Ellenbogen himself was accused of having committed war crimes. He was convicted, given a life sentence, and died in prison three years later.[2]

Of itself, this was a remarkable narrative based on the doctor's sworn testimony, but what particularly caught my eye upon reading Edwin Black's book was the following, which referred to Katzen-Ellenbogen's employment in New Jersey:

> In 1911 Woodrow Wilson became governor of New Jersey.... Katzen-Ellenbogen was asked to become scientific director of the State Village for Epileptics at Skillman, New Jersey.... As the state's leading expert on epilepsy, [he] was asked by Wilson to draft New Jersey's law to sterilize epileptics and defectives.[3]

I was aware that Woodrow Wilson had been governor of New Jersey before being elected president, but had never heard about this American physician, a convicted war criminal no less, who had written a law in my home state that was intended to forcibly sterilize epileptics and other "defectives." My curiosity piqued, I began by researching obscure archival material and other history sources and eventually concluded that much of Dr. Katzen-Ellenbogen's testimony at Dachau either was distorted or totally false, probably in a self-serving effort to impress the tribunal.

My findings about Dr. Katzen-Ellenbogen will be summarized at the very end of this work, for, as it turned out, he played only a minor role on the New Jersey stage, working in the state for little more than one year. Nevertheless, his brief presence loomed as an evil specter over actual events and as I learned more about what happened in New Jersey early in the last century, my focus shifted away from the false narrative of an enigmatic villain to take on a broader perspective. In the process I came to the disturbing realization that many prominent New Jerseyans embraced "social Darwinism," the idea of survival of the fittest applied to humans, and encouraged programs which were used to justify involuntary sterilization of mentally handicapped patients in the United States and also provided a model which led to mass murder in Nazi Germany. Indeed, it seemed to me that New Jersey was not merely a microcosm of what was happening at the same time elsewhere, but served as a crucial proving ground for validating eugenic theory.

So what began as an exploration of the saga of one flawed individual led to a broader awareness of past events in New Jersey, especially as they played out both at Skillman Village for Epileptics and at its related institution, the Vineland Training School For Feeble-minded Girls and Boys, which sometimes was referred to as "The Village of Happiness." It is my hope that the story recounted here will provide a cautionary lesson for our own time—that what may start with good intentions can under special circumstances lead to outrageous violations of human rights.

Perhaps a word of explanation may be appropriate about my book's title, *A Tale of Two Villages*. Of course it is an allusion to Dickens's novel *A Tale of Two Cities*, which concerned social injustices against the backdrop of the French Revolution. However this story is based on fact, not fiction, and the conflagration which it foreshadowed was World War II. "It was the best of times, it was the worst of times." These are the famous opening words of Dickens's *A Tale of Two Cities*. So was it at Vineland and Skillman during much of the early twentieth century. During a period of war and economic depression, and inspired by the emergence of new scientific ideas, well-meaning people attempted to do what they understood would benefit mankind. Subsequent events proved that most of them either were naïve, gullible, or misguided. At the end of Dickens's novel the tragic protagonist Sydney Carton, while on his way to the guillotine, declares: "It is a far, far better thing that I do now than I have ever done. It is a far, far better place that I go to than I have ever known." In that same redemptive spirit, hopefully, our society may have learned from mistakes of the past.

My intention here is not to replicate the extensive literature which already has been written about eugenics theory or to recount in great detail the horrors of the Holocaust, except insofar as they relate to my main theme. Nor does this book focus on the general history of the "villages" at Vineland and Skillman *per se*. Certainly many admirable things occurred at these places as well as at similar institutions that have been documented by others. Rather, my purpose is to concentrate on a single issue—government coerced eugenics based sterilization—a subject that has rarely been discussed in the context of events that played out in the state of New Jersey.

We have advanced a long way from events of nearly a century ago, but in order to progress further we should never lose sight of where we've been—and why.

Moral Treatment

To set the stage for what will come, it is worth considering that throughout history people with mental illness were viewed with fear and misunderstanding and were subjected to social stigmatization or physical punishment. Even those afflicted with epilepsy, "the falling sickness," were lumped together with the insane and the "feeble-minded," as well as with the dregs of society—prostitutes, delinquents, beggars, vagrants, criminals, the homeless. Such people often were treated like wild animals, placed naked or in rags in cages and dungeons and almshouses, neglected, often restrained in chains and lashed into obedience. The cause of madness was variously attributed to divine punishment, possession by demons, phases of the moon, religious ecstasy, or, in Victorian times, even to reading novels. Moreover, the prevailing belief was that the mentally ill had to be driven out of polite society lest they propagate their kind.

But by the end of the eighteenth century there was impetus for change.[4] Imbued with Enlightenment ideas of social justice and the rights of man, there was a growing sense in Europe that these unfortunates should be treated with sympathy and kindness, albeit with firmness. Among the reformers was the French physician Philippe Pinel (1745-1826) who criticized contemporary methods of treatment and famously unshackled imprisoned lunatics: "To detain maniacs in constant seclusion and to load them with chains, to leave them defenseless, to the brutality of underlings.... is a system of

1

superintendence more distinguished for its convenience than for its humanity or its success." Dr. Pinel linked mental illness with social conditions and, along with like-minded colleagues, proposed a psychologically oriented approach that combined reward and punishment in order to promote discipline. This approach became known in England and America as "moral treatment," and one of its tenets was that confinement in a well-ordered asylum was indispensable to humane care.

By the mid-nineteenth century, increasing numbers of mental asylums in England permitted patients to move about freely and engage in simple "therapeutic employment." Advocates pursued their good works with religious zeal, particularly Quakers, who endorsed the virtues of gentleness, and a wholesome way of life. There was a growing sense that some cases, particularly those involving children, were partially remediable with simple schooling. Although such humane impulses were well-intentioned, there also was an element of elitism and condescension. If asylum inmates no longer were physically restrained, they were to be remolded in order to conform with societal norms of behavior, perhaps at the expense of their own individuality.

The patron saint of lunacy reform in mid-nineteenth century America was a former Boston school teacher named Dorothea Dix (1802-1887) who went to England for respite from her own severe depression, and during a four-year stay there was inspired by the burgeoning reform movement. To her, Pinel's work of nearly a century before was "the first great triumph of humanity and skill over ferocity and ignorance." Back in America in 1842, Dorothea Dix became an indefatigable lobbyist, who argued that government should play a central role in providing humane care for all mentally ill persons. Over a fifteen-year period she traveled widely throughout the United States, and everywhere Dorothea Dix looked she found large numbers of insane people in jails or almshouses or wandering about. Dix kept meticulous records, sometimes embellishing the facts, and was skillful in dramatizing her message to legislators: "I come to present the strong claims of suffering humanity." It was a time when there was growing agreement that government should build public institutions to deal with poverty, crime, and insanity, and Dorothea Dix was instrumental in establishing more than thirty state asylums, all of them providing "moral treatment"—and all built according to the design principles of Philadelphia psychiatrist Thomas S. Kirkbride.[5]

Dr. Kirkbride believed that the environment in which mentally ill patients lived could be made an integral part of the treatment, and he promoted a standardized method of asylum construction which became widely known as "The Kirkbride Plan." The basic model called for fortress-like buildings which were placed on large tracts of parkland or in bucolic settings far removed from population centers and suitable for farming. The plan incorporated a linear design with a massive central administrative building and attached radiating residential wings. Public spaces were relatively light and airy, and stone construction was used in order to reduce the risk of fires. During the nineteenth century psychiatry was exclusively practiced within such large custodial institutions, and equally as important as the structural organization was the regimen employed within their walls. It was believed that if asylums were properly constructed and treatment well organized, at least some unfortunates might improve, perhaps even be discharged.

New Jersey lagged behind its neighbors in providing for their "idiots, epileptics and insane poor." The state neither had private asylums nor professional expertise, but, as she already had done elsewhere, Dorothea Dix gathered horror stories about what she saw, and in 1844 testified before New Jersey's legislature. She flattered the legislators for their forward thinking in having already established a study commission which had reported that "mental maladies are as susceptible of cure as corporeal and … when the disease cannot be healed, the suffering may be alleviated." Then Dix appealed to their sense of fairness, declaring that New Jersey was sufficiently prosperous that they could afford to do the "honorable" thing by establishing a state institution to meet the citizens' needs. After her passionate report to the New Jersey legislature, which she called a "memorial," was approved as written, Dorothea Dix was asked to advise about where and how the new facility should be located and run. The result was the state's first "lunatic asylum," which was built in Trenton according to the Kirkbride Plan. The imposing main building could accommodate more than a thousand, but soon became overcrowded, necessitating a second asylum to be opened in 1876 on over seven hundred acres near Morristown. Designed for six hundred patients, within a few years it, too, became overcrowded, and in 1899 a huge addition was built, which was called the New Jersey State Hospital For The Insane.(In 1924 the unsavory name was changed to Greystone Park.)

In 1882 Dorothea Dix, by then a frail invalid in her eighties, moved into a special apartment in the Trenton asylum, which she had planned from the ground up and which she sometimes described as her "first-born" child. She spent her last six years writing letters and still lobbying politicians. Ever modest and self-effacing in life, the name Dorothea Dix is nearly forgotten today, but she was an influential force for good who, as it was said, "gave madness a human face." Even as they proliferated in numbers throughout the country, conditions in the massive Kirkbride buildings deteriorated because of underfunding and understaffing, and gradually the idea of "building as a cure" fell out of favor. What had been intended to be the solution of a social problem became identified as the problem itself. The behemoths were phased out, and the Kirkbride Plan was replaced by a new approach to asylum construction in which buildings still were placed on large tracts of land but were limited to one or two stories and were separated, much like with college campuses.

It Takes a Village

So-called "colonies," which had opened in several European countries during the nineteenth century, impressed visiting Americans such as the wealthy philanthropist William Pryor Letchworth. Upon returning from a seven-month sojourn in 1890, he became an advocate for the mentally ill and epileptics. Letchworth urged that European methods of reform be adopted, and in 1898 he and a colleague, Dr. Frederick Peterson, organized the National Association for the Study of Epilepsy and the Cure and Treatment of Epileptics which several years later affiliated with the newly formed International League Against Epilepsy (ILAE.) Since 1879 a bill had languished in the Ohio Legislature which called for a separate institution for epileptics, but it wasn't passed until 1890. Three years later the first patients were admitted to The Ohio Hospital for Epileptics at Gallipolis and placed in homelike cottages grouped around central administrative buildings on 110 acres of farmland. The antiepileptic medications of the time (bromides, arsenic, and belladonna) were ineffective, and emphasis was placed on peaceful surroundings and therapeutic low-protein diets.

According to an early report, "Many of the patients came from the almshouses, many from the lower walks of life, and were uncouth in manners and dress, filthy in their habits and rude in their conversation. The improvement most noticed by visitors has been the wonderful change in their deportment." However, by the end of the nineteenth century there was growing appreciation that epileptics were different from other categories of "madmen"—many may have required lifelong care, but not all were idiots. Indeed, the list of people of genius who may have been epileptics was long and well known: Julius Caesar, Peter the Great, Fyodor Dostoevsky, Lord Byron, and perhaps even Joan of Arc.

Several similar epileptic colonies soon followed elsewhere in this country. As a result of Letchworth's and Peterson's efforts, in 1896 the Craig Colony for Epileptics opened in Sonyea, New York, forty miles from Rochester on the site of a former Shaker village. Its superintendent described the design of separating patients into small detached cottages as essential because it provided an opportunity for residents to engage in simple trades or farming. Craig Colony's resident pathologist, J.F.Munson noted that "a secluded life of comfort and industry opens to the epileptic prospects of happiness and usefulness which he could not otherwise have, and makes available a great clinical material which will some time or other make possible a solution of this great problem by exposing the underlying cause of disease."[6]

In time the harsh descriptive rhetoric softened so that the insane were vaguely referred to as being feebleminded, and inmates were called children. Rather than asylums, the refuges were referred to as colonies, villages, or schools, where the idea was to create a semblance of normalcy, self-dependent communities whose residents lived and worked in close proximity to staff according to their limited abilities. (Decades later Hillary Clinton metaphorically expressed a similar idea when she adapted the African proverb "It takes a village to raise a child" in order to emphasize our mutual interdependence and the importance of community activism.)

The Perils of Pus

Because the focus of this book is upon New Jersey, at this point it may be useful to provide some historical context by considering a parallel and idiosyncratic phenomenon which flourished in the state during the first quarter of the twentieth century. By then mainstream psychiatry seems to have reached a dead end, as outcomes of "moral treatment" in the large institutions were discouraging. The new "talk treatment" being espoused by Sigmund Freud and his colleagues in Europe was disparaged by many, who considered Freud to be a charlatan. As we shall soon consider, an alternative theory based on eugenics ideology was becoming increasingly favored by many, who believed that mental illness was due to an incurable inherited defect which, if not addressed, inevitably would result in future generations of more defectives.

Many psychiatrists resented psychologists and social workers, who they perceived as challengers to their authority. However, recent medical advances seemed to offer an opportunity for psychiatrists to assume a more influential place in the professional hierarchy. The dawn of bacteriology, based on the work of Pasteur and Koch, suggested that germs might be the cause of many unexplained disorders—perhaps including mental illness. Neurosyphillis (paresis) was due to a spirochete infecting the brain; the Wasserman blood test enabled diagnosis, and Paul Ehrlich's "magic bullet," Salvarsan, promised a cure. Why not take a similar approach with other forms of mental illness? Could psychosis, like syphilitic paresis, be due to a foreign agent? Dr. Adolf Meyer of Johns Hopkins, the most prestigious American psychiatrist during the early twentieth century, believed that all mental activity was based on physiology and its "anatomical substratum." Consistent with this theoretical framework, which Meyer called "psychobiology," occult infections might be a correctable cause of mental illness, and if cure could be achieved there wouldn't be a need for overcrowded, expensive mental institutions. What was needed was a champion willing to lead the way in finding a muscular alternative to the effete psychoanalytic approach or the fatalistic heredity theorists.

Now entered an optimistic new voice from Dorothea Dix's "first born," the New Jersey State Hospital in Trenton.[7] Dr. Henry Cotton, one of Adolf Meyer's former students, was appointed to be superintendent of Trenton State in 1907 after his predecessor was fired because of patient abuse and scandals. Having completed postgraduate studies in Munich, Dr. Cotton had come to reject both psychoanalysis and eugenics theory. About the latter he said, "We are now in a position to say, with reasonable confidence, if not absolute finality, that mental disease *per se* cannot be transmitted from one generation to another." As for Freud, his work was dismissed with the curious remark, "psychoanalysis, in time, will be superceded by gastric analysis." Gastric analysis!

In those days, asylum superintendents were autocrats in white coats who exerted strong control over their institution's policies; but Dr. Cotton was more interested in clinical than administrative matters. To his credit, he drastically reduced the use of restraints at Trenton and increased the number and quality of physicians and nurses, but he was unable to make any significant inroads in treatment outcomes. Henry Cotton gradually came to accept the idea that psychosis was not a disease entity at all, but a symptom of focal low-grade infection lurking unsuspected in the body, as a result of which accumulated toxins acted directly upon brain cells. These pockets of pus needed to be found and extirpated—"surgical bacteriology." Dr. Cotton was not the first to propose this theory, but beginning in 1916 he began pursuing his theory in earnest and quickly became the world's most outspoken proponent of eradicating focal sepsis in order to prevent or cure mental illness, hailed in England as "the new Lister."

The most obvious locus of occult focal infection was the mouth, and Dr. Cotton attacked the problem by removing teeth and tonsils of patients—even if there were no obvious abnormal signs. Similarly, bridges and crowns were removed, and if that didn't do the job, the doctor probed deeper and removed internal organs—gallbladders, spleens, reproductive organs, thyroids. If abdominal X-rays revealed excess retention of fecal matter, or if the patient suffered from constipation, colectomies were performed, with astonishingly high operative mortality between 30 and 40 percent. In one twelve-month period (1919-1920) 6,472 dental extractions were done, an average of ten per admission, as well as 542 tonsillectomies and 79 colon resections. Trenton State's X-ray machine was kept humming, with more than four thousand studies done annually. Between 1918 and 1925, 2,186 major operations were performed, often against the expressed wishes of patients or their families, and not only for psychosis—they were done on children to correct "sexual abnormalities," such as masturbation, in order to prevent insanity. Indicative of Dr. Cotton's misguided sincerity was that he had his wife's and two sons' teeth extracted, even some of his own, and caused one son to have a partial colectomy.

Dr. Cotton claimed impressive clinical results as well as doubling discharge rates and reducing hospital costs. After one lecture at Princeton University, a reporter for the *New York Times* gushed: "At the State Hospital in Trenton, under the brilliant leadership of the medical director, Dr. Henry A. Cotton, there is on foot the most searching, aggressive and profound scientific investigation that has as yet been made of the whole field of mental and nervous disorders.... there is hope, high hope ... for the future." In 1921 Dr. Hubert Work, the president of the American Medical Association, declared that Trenton State was one of the country's "great institutions [a tribute] to the public mind of the people of New Jersey, a composite of their social morals, their charity and Christianity in its broadest sense, and it is as well a monument to the most advanced civilization of her people." The president of the New Jersey Medical Society, Henry Costill, proclaimed, "Dr. Cotton has built a foundation for the benefit of the health of the people of which each succeeding generation will reap the benefit and generations to come will rise up and call him blessed."[8]

Small wonder that wealthy madmen and women from all over flocked toTrenton to be cured by the great man—ready to sacrifice teeth, tonsils, and colons in a desperate search for sanity. Their numbers exceeded the hospital's capacity, and Dr. Cotton was obliged to open a small private hospital (The Charles Hospital) nearby in order to accommodate the well-paying customers. Dr. Cotton was a superb self-promoter, but by 1922 there were some within the profession who began criticizing the Trenton approach. The results seemed too good to be true—an 85 percent cure rate of psychosis, fourteen hundred inmates discharged "cured" over a four-year period, average length of hospital stay reduced from ten to three months. It was one thing to bring psychiatry into the medical mainstream, but if Cotton was correct, some feared that it might be demoted to a subdivision of dentistry or surgery.

The director self-righteously defended his work from critics, whom he usually chose to ignore. When asked to explain forty-nine deaths in a sequence of 148 total colectomies, unabashed, he rationalized that many of these patients had "end-stage" psychosis, so radical surgery was done as a last desperate chance to save them. Faced with a rising tide of criticism, in 1925 Cotton finally agreed to permit an independent investigation. The results were devastating—not only was record keeping at Trenton sloppy, but the benefits of surgery had been vastly exaggerated. However, his influential supporter, Adolf Meyer, suppressed the findings of the report that he had commissioned. If anything, Dr. Cotton became even more radical in his crusade. Now it was insufficient to remove only infected teeth; all teeth had to be extracted before he would proceed to "detoxication" or "defocalization" surgery—an elevated white blood cell count was sufficient proof of infection.

After his death Dr.Cotton's findings were discredited, but prophylactic dental extractions and tonsillectomies continued unabated for decades. Resecting focal infection was merely one approach to treating madness that was being employed at Trenton and elsewhere. Other futile fads included colonic irrigations, diathermy, hydrotherapy, fever therapy with malaria or typhoid vaccines, inducing convulsions with insulin, metrazol, or camphor, and, worst of all, lobotomies—all endorsed by scientists engaged in a Quixotic quest for a biologic cure. Henry Cotton's career in Trenton was idiosyncratic, and the theory of focal infection as the cause of mental illness would not have lasting effects. The reaction of most of his colleagues was negative, but most disturbing is that during the 1920s no one saw fit to challenge Henry Cotton's right to prescribe aggressive, unproven surgery. Nor was there any discussion about any ethical considerations of forcing such treatments upon unwilling patients. Nevertheless, Dr. Cotton's general approach was not entirely an aberration. It reflected organized medicine's paternalism—physicians presumed that they knew better than others and had no qualms experimenting on patients without permission or even despite objections, all for the sake of science.

Henry Cotton may have been deluded, but he was not a racist. In effect, the debacle in Trenton can be understood as an example of the parable of the emperor's new clothes—few dared to criticize the medical mighty. Even the imperious Adolf Meyer was timid when confronted with his self-assured former student. When the surgical carnage ceased with Cotton's unexpected death from a heart attack in 1933 at age 54, Dr. Meyer held back public criticism. Evidently he was as much concerned with protecting his own as his protégé's reputation. He eulogized Henry Cotton as "one of the most stimulating figures of our generation.... a remarkable example of energy, purpose and whole heartedness."

In retrospect, this saga of Dr. Henry Cotton seems ludicrous, but it exemplifies how primitive medical science was less than a century ago. Of far greater importance than the aberrant germ theory of insanity was the parallel emergence of eugenics during the early years of the twentieth century, for if the source of madness could not be directly cut out, there seemed to be a possibility that it could be cut off.

Bad Seeds

The late nineteenth century English mathematician Francis Galton used statistical correlations to study the inheritance of intelligence and in 1883 coined the term "eugenics" (Greek: good in birth). He introduced the idea of selective breeding for the betterment of mankind, which was partially based on the theories of his cousin, Charles Darwin, whose study on human evolution, *The Origin of the Species*, had been published in 1859. Although Darwin greatly admired his cousin's work, he thought that the idea of hereditary improvement of humans would be impractical. Galton defined eugenics as the scientific study of racial improvement and proposed that gifted subjects should be encouraged to reproduce. He held that personality characteristics, including intelligence, are just as heritable as physical characteristics. Like many others of his time, he believed in the relative superiority of Europeans compared to what he called "the lower races." Galton wrote that Jews were capable only of "parasitism" upon the civilized nations and that the behavior of negroes was "so childish, stupid and simpleton-like, as frequently to make me ashamed of my own species." These reprehensible words notwithstanding, it's unlikely that either Darwin or Galton would have approved of government coercion of the principles of natural selection that would occur in Germany a half century later. In his book *Hereditary Genius* (1869) Francis Galton wrote:

Each generation has enormous power over the natural gifts of those that follow, and I maintain that it is a duty we owe to humanity to investigate the range of that power, and to exercise it in a way that, without being unwise towards ourselves, shall be most advantageous to future inhabitants of the earth.[9]

Eugenics was supported by a small but influential group of scientists, politicians, and intellectuals, most of whom were white, male, Anglo-Saxon Protestants. It was taught at leading universities and discussed in standard texts of human heredity. It's been suggested that if religion was the opium of the masses, eugenics was the religion of the aristocrats whose elitist social and political agendas were based on the belief that Western civilization was in danger of committing racial suicide as a result of the rapid reproduction of the unfit coupled with a decline in the birthrate of the supposedly "better" classes. As a solution, they proposed a program of "positive" and "negative" eugenics—positive because they encouraged increased reproduction of better-educated, supposedly superior people ("like breeding a race of thoroughbreds"); negative by limiting the numbers of the unfit through immigration restriction, laws to prohibit interracial marriage, and government policies favoring compulsory sterilization,

Many famous people agreed. In 1910 Winston Churchill expressed his support for a law that proposed compulsory sterilization for the "feeble-minded." It didn't pass. Churchill once told a group of eugenicists that Britain's 120,000 feebleminded persons, if possible, should be segregated (in colonies).... "so that their curse died with them and was not transmitted to future generations." George Bernard Shaw wrote: "Plutocratic inbreeding has produced a weakness of character.... Being cowards we defeat natural selection under cover of philanthropy: being sluggards, we neglect artificial selection under cover of delicacy and morality." H.G. Wells urged sterilization of society's "failures," whether they wanted it or not. In 1913 former President Teddy Roosevelt said, "We have no business to permit the perpetuation of citizens of the wrong type." And who were the wrong type? Margaret Sanger thought that she knew. The birth control crusader and proto-feminist saw eugenics practice as a way to lower the birth rate of such undesirables as "Hebrews, Slavs, Catholics and Negroes." Her slogan was "More children for the fit; less for the unfit." Grounds for sterilization included such categories as immorality, masturbation, hereditary deafness, and blindness. There were pragmatic issues as well—how much money was being spent to keep unproductive cripples and degenerates alive? Sanger deplored "reckless procreation" and "indiscriminate breeding" and warned that "human weeds" were choking the "garden of humanity." She declared that birth control and eugenics were allied, both seeking a single end. Equally outspoken as Margaret Sanger was the gentleman sportsman and conservationist Madison Grant. (His father Dr. Gabriel Grant of Newark, New Jersey was a surgeon in the Second New Jersey Volunteers who during the Civil War was awarded the Medal of Honor for bravery.) This builder of the Bronx Zoo who was instrumental in saving California's Redwood trees feared that like the American Indian and the buffalo, the great Nordic race was facing extinction. To him, preservation efforts should be directed not only at eradicating unfit individuals, but at groups who were racially unfit. Deplorable as these ideas seem today, most eugenicists earnestly hoped to improve the lot of mankind. These supposedly sophisticated people thought that at stake was the preservation of the human species—or at least their kind of human species.[10]

Cold Spring Harbor:
The Epicenter of Eugenics

The American Breeders Association (ABA) was one of the first eugenics organizations in the United States. Founded in 1903 by agricultural breeders and academic biologists, it was funded by the wealth of the Carnegie, Rockefeller and Harriman families. In 1906 the ABA established a Committee on Eugenics that was designed to emphasize the value to society of "superior blood" and the menace of "inferior blood." It appeared self-evident to many of these people that qualities such as intelligence, mental illness, work ethic, criminality, and poverty were inherited and it seemed logical that if undesirable groups were prevented from reproducing, it would benefit society. The organization's leader, Charles B. Davenport, defined eugenics as "the science of the improvement of the human race by better breeding." To Davenport, a member of the National Academy of Sciences, "heredity stands as the one great hope of the human race," and a practical solution was at hand for sterilization could "dry up the springs that feed the torrent of defective and degenerate protoplasm."

> The general program of the eugenicist is clear—it is to improve the race by inducing young people to make a more reasonable selection of marriage mates; to fall in love intelligently. It also includes the control by the state of the

propagation of the mentally incompetent. It does not imply the destruction of the unfit either before or after birth.[11.]

The epicenter of the eugenics movement was an estate at Cold Spring Harbor, Long Island, where Davenport's associate Harry H. Laughlin directed the Eugenics Record Office (ERO), which was financed primarily by Mary Harriman, widow of the railroad baron E. H. Harriman. The idea was to put the study of human traits on a firm, quantitative basis and the ERO served as a clearinghouse for data concerning bloodlines and family traits. By 1924 its files contained records of 750,000 individuals and families based on interviews performed by trained field workers. Laughlin also headed a Committee on Sterilization, which included such influential scientists as Alexander Graham Bell, William Castle, and Adolf Meyer as consultants. Chaired by Bleeker Van Wagenen, a wealthy philanthropist from South Orange, New Jersey, the group was charged with finding the best practical way of "purging the blood of the American people of the handicapping and deteriorating influences of … anti-social classes."

How many people did the zealots of good breeding expect to "fix"? Some estimated that the "clearly unfit" numbered close to a million; borderline cases added another seven million or so. Harry Laughlin suggested an even higher number—perhaps eleven million—if one included those who superficially appeared to be normal. The ERO report concluded that approximately 10 percent of the American population "primarily through inherent defect and weakness, are an economic and moral burden on the 90percent and a constant danger to the national and racial life." But, as they saw it, the menace could be averted by cutting off the defective people's capacity to pass their defective genes to their offspring.

Vineland: "The Village of Happiness"

As early as 1845 New Jersey State Senator Stephen Garrison began promoting the idea of establishing a school for mentally retarded children, but it wasn't until 1887 that his son, Rev. Stephen Olin Garrison, who had a retarded son, opened a small school in his own home. The next year it was moved to a forty-acre campus in nearby Vineland. Initially it was called *The Vineland Training School For Feeble-Minded Girls and Boys*; five years later the name was changed to *The New Jersey Training School*. Training was individualized so that students were taught "what they ought to know and can make use of when they become men and women in years." S. O. Garrison didn't merely want a school but dreamt of a self-sustaining "village" where the retarded might live safely—a humane version of the "cottage plan" or farm colony that was coming to dominate thinking about custodial care. In 1888 Garrison convinced the legislature to open the "Vineland State Institution for Feeble-minded Women" across the street from the training school. Five years later, visiting educator Professor Earl Barnes declared:

> To me an institution for the feebleminded is a human laboratory and a garden where unfortunate children are cared for, protected and loved while they unconsciously whisper to us syllable by syllable the secrets of the soul's growth. It may very well be that the most ignorant will teach us most.[12]

Others saw it as a way to relieve the state from perpetuating a race of feebleminded paupers. When Garrison died in 1900 he was replaced as superintendent by an enthusiastic twenty-nine-year-old, Edward R. Johnstone, who would remain in this position until his death in 1945. His creed for Vineland was "Happiness First, All Else Follows." Children who had been rejected by the world could be accepted in what Johnstone called this "village of happiness.". Others lauded the energetic "Vineland spirit" that permeated the place. E. R.Johnstone saw his work as a great challenge. It also was his delight, and he exulted in his good fortune, "Where in all the wide, wide world ... is there such a wonderful opportunity within such a small compass, covering such a stretch of time, and directed and practically controlled by one man—the Superintendent?" In 1908 the Training School's principal reported to the Board of Managers:

> The Vineland Training School is the one institution in the world where such a comprehensive plan as we have can be carried out.... It will be a sin to humanity if we fail to seize the opportunity..... Both in Europe and America money and energy is being wasted in an attempt to make "mental cripples" run intellectual foot races.... Let us then cease to torment our defectives with abstractions and devote ourselves to developing their minds in interesting occupations.[13]

Professor Johnstone's program included studying the causes and management of mental retardation, and toward this end, in 1906 he hired psychologist Henry Herbert Goddard, a former college football coach, in order to establish a Psychological Research Laboratory. It was the first in the country dedicated exclusively to studying mental disorders. Dr. Goddard, wanting a way of identifying which students potentially could learn and which could not, traveled to seven European countries to consult with experts. He was not impressed by what he found, but while in Paris he met Alfred Binet, who, with Theodore Simon, had developed a method of testing intelligence in children. Binet had devised the scale as a rough empirical guide for identifying mildly retarded children and not as a device for ranking normal children: "They do not define anything innate or permanent. We may not designate what they measure as 'intelligence.'"

Henry Goddard brought the Simon-Binet tests home, had them translated, and in 1910 began using these so-called "IQ tests" in order to numerically classify the children at Vineland. The degree of retardation was determined by the difference between the mental age attained and the present chronological age. At first Goddard was skeptical about the test's utility but was surprised to find close correlation of scores with intuitive observations made by his team of social workers, who had gathered anthropological and genealogic information. Preliminary studies indicated that 65 percent of the Vineland children had "the hereditary taint." In order to standardize results, the work was expanded to include thousands of presumably normal children in local public schools. When Goddard distributed 22,000 copies of the test throughout the country, he launched a national movement to measure innate intellectual ability using IQ tests. In advocating for wide testing, Goddard departed from Binet's intention to use IQ tests only to assess children with specific learning problems. A 1916 revision by Lewis M. Terman, who dreamed of a rational society that would allocate professions by IQ scores, led to the now familiar Stanford-Binet version. The premise of hereditarians like Goddard and Terman was that environmental, social, and economic factors had negligible effects upon intelligence, and that IQ scores identified people and groups for an inevitable station in life. They believed that if allowed to proliferate unchecked, those at the low end of the intelligence spectrum endangered American stock. Goddard argued that such people should be denied entrance into the country and that those already here should be segregated in institutions where they could be made happy by catering to their limits and, above all, prevented from breeding.

Dr. Goddard was intrigued by the pedigree of one student, whom he called by the pseudonym "Deborah Kallikak." Deborah had been admitted to the Training School at Vineland in 1897 at age eight; now age 22, her IQ test indicated that she had the mental ability of a nine-year-old. Field workers were able to trace Deborah's family roots back six generations and discovered that in 1776 Martin Kallikak, an upstanding Quaker, had sex with a "feebleminded tavern wench" who lived in Piney Woods, a rural settlement in central New Jersey. She bore an illegitimate boy from this union of whose 480 subsequent offspring, only forty-six were considered to be "normals"— among the others there were an inordinate number of drunkards, social misfits, alcoholics, epileptics, and other "degenerates." On the other hand, when Martin Kallikak married a woman of "his own quality," later generations were deemed to be "respectable" judges, professors, and public servants. Goddard had coined the surname "Kallikak" from Greek words *kallos* and *kakos*, meaning "beauty" and "bad," and his explanation of this genealogy was revealing:

> The foregoing charts and text tell a story as instructive as it is amazing. We have here a family of good English blood of the middle class, settling upon the original land purchased from the proprietors of the state in Colonial times, and throughout four generations maintaining a reputation for honor and respectability of which they are justly proud. Then a scion of this family, in an unguarded moment, steps aside from the paths of rectitude and with the help of a feeble-minded girl, starts a line of mental defectives that is truly appalling.[14]

Dr. Goddard claimed that no amount of education or good environment could change a feebleminded individual into a normal one, "any more than it can change a red-haired stock into a black-haired stock." He concluded his analysis by noting that "for the low-grade idiot, the loathsome unfortunate that may be seen in our institutions, some have proposed the lethal chamber. But humanity is steadily tending away from the possibility of that method, and there is no probability that it will ever be practiced." But if the "lethal chamber" was not the answer, Goddard did have some alternate suggestions:

> Segregation through colonization seems in the present state of our knowledge to be the ideal and perfectly satisfactory method. Sterilization may be accepted as a makeshift, as a help to solve the problem because the conditions have become so intolerable. But this must at present be regarded only as a

temporary, for before it can be extensively practiced, a great deal must be learned about the effects of the operation and about the laws of human inheritance.[15]

Henry Goddard's findings were published in 1912 in a book written for a lay audience, *The Kallikak Family: A Study in the Heredity of Feeble-Mindedness*. It was an instant best seller and, in time, a notorious classic work in modern psychology. The book seemed to confirm the earlier work of New York prison reformer Richard Dugdale, who in 1877 had published *The Jukes: A Study in Crime, Pauperism, Disease and Heredity*. Dugdale's emphasis had been on hereditary criminality, while Goddard's was more on feeblemindedness; both books, however, created sensations, and the fictitious names "Jukes" and "Kallikaks" became forever linked in the public vernacular. Dr. Goddard had coined the term "moron" as a category to be distinguished by their IQ scores from lower-grade "idiots" and "imbeciles," and as a result of the popularity of his book, Deborah Kallikak was said to be "the most famous moron in the world." Although superficially morons might appear to be normal, Goddard warned, they were promiscuous, often had illegitimate children, frequented saloons and whorehouses, and filled state prisons. He explained that the human family contained stocks, like the Kallikaks, that "breed as true as anything in plant or animal life" and that it was the moral obligation of the intelligent portion of society to enforce eugenic theory and control this "menace" by limiting the immigration and the propagation of morons. To him, "Democracy is a method for arriving at a benevolent aristocracy," where the wisest, most intelligent, and most humane dictate what is best for the general welfare.

To do the primary research, Henry Goddard was assisted by a group of social workers who had been trained at Cold Spring. Among them was an idealistic researcher, Elizabeth S. Kite, who, like Goddard, was raised in the Quaker tradition and shared the same puritanical convictions. Being skilled in French, it was she who translated Binet's work and performed much of the primary field work which Goddard interpreted. In 1913, Elizabeth Kite, in a report of her own findings titled *The Pineys*, characterized residents of New

Jersey's Pine Barrens region, just North of Vineland, as "lazy, lustful and cunning"—"sowers of wild oats." For two years she'd traveled through the backwoods in a horse-drawn wagon, interviewing the locals, asking leading questions, and then scoring people as "normal" or "feebleminded" according to behavior described by others, even of people long dead. Ms. Kite justified deviations from Binet's scientific protocol on the basis that working at Vineland provided her with special insight. As she saw it, the crucial question was whether or not a subject demonstrated good sense—"armed with this central thought the Vineland field worker goes forth." It is easy to appreciate how, "armed" with her own agenda, she could find whatever it was that she was looking for.

Elizabeth Kite concluded, "The time has come for us as an enlightened community to set about clearing up these 'backdoors of our civilization' and to save from the worst form of contagion what remains of moral health in our rising generations." Alerted and alarmed, New Jersey's Governor James T. Fielder recommended that the Pine Barrens region be segregated in order to preserve the health and safety of the state's citizens from this menace. When the governor visited the area he was shocked at the number of inbred Pineys who led "lawless and scandalous lives, till they have become a race of imbeciles, criminals and defectives." Before long the word "Piney" was being used widely as a pejorative.

In 1910, E. R. Johnstone and Goddard were invited by officials at Ellis Island to observe their procedures and advise ways to help the Public Health Service in "recognizing and detaining more of the mental defectives." Congress was eager to keep "undesirables" out of the country, and confronted with five thousand or more coming each day, the dozen inspecting physicians at Ellis Island were overwhelmed. Elizabeth Kite and several other "Vineland experts" were sent to help, and they began by observing passing immigrants for any visible evidence of mental disorder; the suspects were given Binet tests. Sometimes an interpreter was provided, but it didn't seem to matter much if immigrants couldn't read English. It was found that the Vineland team members were far more likely to diagnosis feeblemindedness than the Public Health doctors. Goddard explained the disparity this way: "The comparison simply shows what experts can do" and added that it was impossible for the uninitiated to understand how the real expert does his work. Vineland's experts reported that 79 percent of Italians, 83 percent of Jews and 87 percent of Russians were "feebleminded." Even after Goddard manipulated the data, he noted, "We cannot escape the general conclusion that these immigrants were of surprisingly low intelligence." He attributed some of the phenomenon to the changing character of recent immigration from Europe: "We are now getting the poorest of each race."

When the United States entered the Great War against Germany, Superintendent Johnstone offered Vineland's full assistance to the War Department so that "The Village of Happiness" became the planning center of how to study army recruits. Using Goddard's techniques, they reported that more than half of the soldiers met the definition of morons; for black recruits it was 87 percent. In truth the IQ tests were done crudely and unfairly, but the results seemed to substantiate popular stereotypes. In the preface to his book about the Kallikaks, Henry Goddard offered this caveat:

> If the reader is inclined to the view that we must have called a great many people feeble-minded who were not so, let him be assured that this is not the case. On the contrary, we have preferred to err on the other side, and we have not marked people feeble-minded unless the case was such that we could substantiate it beyond a reasonable doubt.[16]

Then came this condescending revelation:

> To the scientific reader we would say that the data presented here are, we believe, accurate to a high degree. It is true that we have made rather dogmatic statements and have drawn conclusions that do not seem scientifically warranted from the data. We have done this because it seems necessary to make these statements and conclusions for the benefit of the lay reader and it was impossible to present in this book all of the data that would substantiate them.

Skillman Village for Epileptics

From the time of Vineland's beginning, teachers complained that epileptic students sometimes disrupted the routine when they convulsed. Superintendent Garrison suggested that it would be desirable to have a separate facility for epileptics along the lines of Bethel, a famous "Epileptic Colony" in Bielefeld, Germany. In this country, Craig Colony's resident pathologist, J. F. Munson, had distinguished between institutions for epileptics and those for the insane or feebleminded, noting that unlike the latter, epileptics in all probability would live and die with their affliction. He estimated that only 3 to 5 percent of epileptics would ever be cured and argued that they should be institutionalized for life on "farm colonies."

> The epileptic needs care, because of the effect of the disease upon his life in the outside world, making him an objectionable and dependent member of society.... in one way and another, the disease places its indelible mark on him... ultimate dementia is the future of most epileptics.... No one who has witnessed an epileptic seizure will forget the horror and perhaps terror with which it inspires them. The sight of an individual stricken from his normal state to the level of a groveling, inarticulate mass of flesh is one which few can witness with equanimity. Even to those who have been in the work for years, the seizures never lose their horror.... His

disposition and, as time goes on, his mental deterioration, make him hard to get along with; he is irritable and unruly; and carelessness in personal habits makes him an unpleasant member of the family.

The epileptic coming to the institution should come with the expectation of remaining permanently and with the realization that the institution has been created to make for him a place apart from the outside world where he may pass the remainder of his life both happily and usefully. The realization of such an ideal can only be accomplished by separating the epileptic from all other dependents, leaving the institution entirely free to satisfy their needs. The atmosphere of such an institution must be on the one hand one of homelikeness and comfort, and on the other, of quiet industry. The buildings must be such as to withdraw the suggestion of institutionalism and there must be plentiful opportunity for work. And since the institution is apart from the outside world, there must be provision for education, amusement and religious instruction, in every respect a complete village.[17]

In 1898, with the backing of the state medical society, New Jersey's legislature approved $15,000 to establish a State Village for Epileptics at Skillman, a few miles north of Princeton. Adjacent farms comprising about eight hundred acres were purchased, and in December of that year the first seven inmates, the farmer, the cook, the handyman, and the administrator all moved in and occupied one large house. When Skillman's first superintendent, former pathologist Dr. Henry M. Weeks, resigned in December 1907 to take a better-paying job in Pennsylvania, he was replaced by his thirty-two-year-old son, Dr. David F. Weeks, who continued in this role for more than two decades.

In his annual report to Skillman's Board of Managers for 1911, David Weeks noted that a "psychologic research department" had been established at The Village in October of the previous year, and since then all patients were receiving a variety of special tests as developed by Dr. Goddard. Analysis of 177 "pedigrees" of Skillman patients appeared to establish a hereditary linkage between feeblemindedness and epilepsy. The loose diagnostic criteria used by Skillman's field workers included as epileptics people with a variety of unrelated conditions, and their conclusions were based on crude data sampling and faulty assumptions. These included that the children of alcoholic parents are likely to be "tainted" and that "neurotic" conditions are more closely related to epilepsy than to feeblemindedness.

Dr. Weeks acknowledged that his studies were only in their infancy but believed that in due time they would support the inheritance theory. He reported that 5 to 10 percent of epileptics were of sound mind; 18 to 20 percent were insane and 70 to 80 percent had "a mental disablement to some degree." Like Charles Davenport, he believed that epilepsy and feeblemindedness were manifestations of a common inherited "absence of a protoplasmic factor that determines complete nervous development." Concerning prevention, speaking at a state medical meeting in 1911 on "What New Jersey Is Doing For The Epileptic," Dr. Weeks remarked, "The key lies in the restricted use of alcohol, the prevention of the spread of venereal diseases, segregation or sterilization, thus making impossible the multiplication of defectives."[18]

Cold Spring Harbor, on Long Island, may have been the administrative center of the eugenics movement, but New Jersey was its major clinical laboratory, where eugenics theory was tested and validated. Henry Goddard at Vineland and David Weeks at Skillman and their colleagues, working in close collaboration with Charles Davenport and Harry Laughlin, published and lectured on their conjoint work. Dr. Weeks reported that about one quarter of New Jersey's epileptics lived at Skillman, another quarter were in other institutions and schools, and about half were at large in the community. He predicted that a policy of mandatory segregation and selective sterilization would result in a 75 percent reduction of insanity, feeblemindedness, epilepsy, and dipsomania after two generations. Moreover, with proper adherence to this program, within four decades an institution like Skillman probably would provide ample accommodation for all the remaining defectives.

The Indiana Plan

In 1897, Dr. A. J. Oschner of Chicago had performed the first vasectomy in the United States as a supposed remedy for prostate problems, but to many physicians concerned with crime and degeneracy, the procedure also could be done as a more humane alternative to castration as a punishment for sexual offenders. In 1899, Harry Clay Sharp, chief physician at the Indiana State Reformatory, began performing vasectomies on "idiots and low grade imbeciles" whose "obscene habits," such as masturbation, to his mind were the cause of their degeneracy. Other American doctors shared the idea that surgical castration on certain criminals and deviants should be permitted to both punish and prevent them from committing future crimes. After performing several dozen punitive vasectomies, Dr. Sharp adopted the eugenic idea that sterilization was a "rational means of eradicating from our midst a most dangerous and hurtful class.... Radical solutions are necessary." All told, he performed 450 vasectomies on incarcerated men in his charge, reporting that the procedure had "a decided effect on the centers of self-restraint," that it brought with it "increased will power" and provided "a gift of health ... and surplus energy."[19]

Prodded by the appropriately named Dr. Sharp, in 1907 Indiana enacted the first law that provided for mandatory sterilization of "confirmed criminals, idiots, imbeciles and rapists" when recommended by a board of medical experts. Dr. Sharp explained, "idiots, imbeciles and degenerate criminals are prolific, and their defects are transmissible ... so we owe it not only to ourselves but to the future of our race and nations to see that the defective and diseased do not multiply." Dr. Sharp's list of candidates included "the rake, the roué, the neurotic, the erotic, the sexual pervert [and] the reformed prostitute." (Of interest to New Jerseyans: after serving in World War I, Dr. Sharp finished his career as director of a Veterans Administration hospital in New Jersey, dying there in 1940.)

Colorado's Dr. Hubert Work, president of the American Medico-Psychological Association, agreed with Indiana's approach with the caveat, "Our attitude as superintendents must be that of physicians, alienists, political economists, sociologists and through it all humanitarians." Other states soon followed Indiana's lead due to the work of determined public officials and an absence of opposition—New Jersey was the sixth.

New Jersey's Sterilization Law

Henry Goddard had written, "It is the moron type that makes for our great problems," and if idiocy and epilepsy were due to an inherited bad seed which, in turn, was linked with criminal behavior, poverty, and promiscuity, there was a relatively simple solution available:

> In recent years surgeons have discovered another method which has many advantages. This is ... sometimes incorrectly referred to as asexualization. It is more properly spoken of as sterilization.... The results are generally permanent and sure.[20]

Goddard had some reservations about enforced sterilization as was being done in Indiana and California, but these could easily be overcome. Many years later, he recalled how at an unspecified institution and state, "twelve big boys were sterilized. Not one complained. They laughed about it a little." It was so easy to talk the boys into anything: "They love to be talked to, questioned, to be handled and to be 'treated.' In one institution eighty children were given spinal punctures for Wassermans. Not one child made any fuss."[21]

In January 1910, E. R. Johnstone formed a Committee on Provision for the Feebleminded for the purpose of creating public interest in the matter and proposing legislation. The committee, which included

Johnstone and Van Wagenen from Vineland, Skillman's Dr. Weeks, and two others met at Vineland and five hundred dollars was set aside to defray expenses. Letters were sent to enlist parents or guardians of inmates who, in turn, networked with friends and lobbied legislators and the governor. They did their work well, for once the politicians "learned the facts" they were generous with financial support both for Vineland and Skillman. The legislature previously had passed laws prohibiting marriage of the insane (1904) and requiring medical examinations in public school to detect feeblemindedness (1909). Now special classes would be required in every school district where ten or more children were found to lag three years behind normal, and it was time for laws to be enacted concerning institutionalization and sterilization, as in other states.

An Act to Authorize and Provide for the Sterilization of Feeble-minded (Including Idiots, Imbeciles and Morons) Epileptics, Rapists, Certain Criminals and Other Defectives was introduced to New Jersey's legislature on February 27, 1911.[22] It passed the House by 33 ayes to 6 noes, the Senate 12 ayes to 0 noes, and on April 21, 1911, Governor Woodrow Wilson signed the bill into law. The statute required a three-member Board of Examiners of Feebleminded, Epileptics and other Defectives, which included a surgeon and a neurologist in order to review each case. The operation (vasectomy, tubal ligation or salpingectomy) could be performed by any qualified surgeon without liability.

At a public meeting held the next year, Vineland's Superintendent Johnstone boasted, "The Governor couldn't get our sterilization law fast enough to sign it. He signed it the day it came on his desk for fear that a delegation would come up and advocate it's not being signed."[23] More likely, Woodrow Wilson was a true believer. The former president of Princeton and future president of the United States, who served as governor for only two years, evidently understood the sterilizing law to be for human betterment, and he expressed his support for preventing "citizens of the wrong type" from having children.

Eugenics Euphoria

In 1912 New Jersey's eugenicists were flush with success over how easily they'd succeeded in passing their sterilization law. Henry Goddard's book about the Kallikaks was attracting worldwide interest, and Vineland's Research Group had published more than one hundred articles concerning the causes and consequences of mental deficiency. That June the annual meeting of the National Association for the Study of Epilepsy and the Care and Treatment of Epileptics was held at Vineland. The presidential address, delivered by Dr. W. T. Shanahan, superintendent at the Craig Colony for Epileptics in Sonyea, New York, was titled "A Plea For a Moderate Conservatism in the Care and Treatment of Epileptics." Dr. Shanahan began by acknowledging "the good work" that was being done in the field, but cautioned:

> Even if it were possible not only to enact laws for sterilization of neuropaths, but also to enforce them, nobody today would be in a position to tell whether or not it would be desirable, or, on the whole, profitable for the human race to do so. Obtaining broad-based public support would be "absolutely necessary … if eugenics is to accomplish anything in its field…. Optimism is an excellent thing, but that alone cannot overturn public opinion of centuries standing.[24]

Dr. Shanahan declared that the "social danger of the epileptic" was gradually being recognized and that the appropriate solution was permanent segregation: "To bring this about to the desired degree, we must continue to exert our best efforts toward having the public fully realize that such a procedure [segregation] is for the best good of all concerned." Although Shanahan was not talking specifically about sterilization, the Vineland and Skillman eugenicists were in no mood to heed words of restraint.

That same summer the First International Eugenics Congress was held in London, and a major speech was delivered by Bleecker Van Wagenen, a trustee of the Vineland Training School, who chaired the ABA's Committee on Sterilization. Van Wagenen declared that the American technique of surgical sterilization was the best approach and was being done in several states. His report was enthusiastically received, and in the Congress's concluding speech Major Leonard Darwin, Charles Darwin's son, predicted that just as with his father's work during the previous century, eugenics theory would meet resistance. However, he hoped that "the 20th century will.... be known in the future as the century when the eugenics ideal is accepted as part of the creed of civilization." Leonard Darwin concluded, "We shall conquer in time," and he received a standing ovation from the five hundred celebrity guests.[25]

In September 1912, Van Wagenen, Johnstone, and Weeks were in Zurich for the annual meeting of the International League Against Epilepsy. At this conference, Dr. Weeks was elected president of the newly formed ILAE and before returning home traveled throughout Europe to inspect epileptic institutions. No doubt the New Jersey delegates were delighted by their recent warm reception in London and were in an expansive mood, prepared to tell the world what they knew. At the conference Dr. H. M. Carey of Spring City, Pa., speaking about "Compulsory Segregation and Sterilization of the Feeble-Minded and Epileptic," noted that a resolution at a recent meeting of the Chicago Medical Society which endorsed compulsory segregation and sterilization had failed to pass only because the female delegates opposed it. Dr. Carey advised segregation first, followed by vasectomy or castration, and he cautioned that the program must be zealously pursued and made compulsory. "Only a short time ago, we were asking for permission to sterilize certain individuals. Today we beg not for this privilege, but demand that laws be passed compelling its application."[26] To this, Dr. Shanahan responded:

> The subject needs a great deal more study before we will be in a position to have the facts to present to the general public to convince them of the necessity of controlling the propagation of the race ... I feel that we all must honestly come to the conclusion that the time is not ripe as yet to enforce such laws.

Dr. Carey backed off, explaining:

> There is a little confusion concerning segregation and sterilization. I agree that the time is not ripe for a compulsory sterilization act which will include everything. That is absolutely impossible at this time, but I do think—in our own State (Pennsylvania) particularly, we should have a compulsory segregation law.

Then it was New Jersey's turn to comment. Vineland's E. R. Johnstone remarked that public opinion in the state had swung strongly in favor of the eugenicist approach:

> That is the spirit of the legislature of New Jersey, and the people of New Jersey. I believe today, man for man, [we] know more about the problem of the feeble-minded than any state in the Union.... the Legislature itself seems to have shown greater signs of knowledge respecting this matter. All they asked for was a few facts.... just as soon as it was known that the Committee on Provision stood for the legislation which was offered, it went through without any question at all.[27]

Professor Johnstone added that although New Jersey had a mandatory sterilization law, "I do not think that any of us want now to enforce [it] straight ahead from start to finish." He preferred to use persuasion and noted that at Vineland during the previous two years they had asked the parents of twenty inmates for permission to castrate; most were "very well-to-do and wise enough to see the need of it." (I could find no evidence that these voluntary procedures actually were implemented.) The parents of each of these twenty patients agreed to the procedure, and when Johnstone described how parents of feeble-minded and epileptic patients had been effective lobbyists accounting for unprecedented legislative appropriations, the audience applauded.

Bleecker Van Wagenen was the last respondent to Dr. Carey's paper, and he reemphasized that not only should all states have segregation and sterilization laws, but these should include a stipulation that once institutionalized an epileptic patient cannot leave unless permission has been approved both by the institution's superintendent and by the governor. He modestly noted that his ABA eugenics research committee had gathered a great deal of epidemiologic information: "We know more, perhaps, than most any of you know of the specific history of a good many cases ... but we don't have enough yet to generalize."

Judicial Restraint

But New Jersey's sterilization law was short-lived, for even as Vineland's leaders were exulting in Europe, a test case from Skillman was being reviewed in New Jersey's courts. On May 31, 1912, Dr. Weeks and Skillman's Board of Examiners reviewed the case of Alice Smith, an inmate at the Village since 1902 who had not had a seizure in five years. When they advised salpingectomy for prevention of procreation, their decision was appealed by the patient's state-appointed attorney. After two lower court reviews it was taken up by the state's Supreme Court, which on November 18, 1913, unanimously declared that New Jersey's sterilization law represented cruel and unusual violation of the equal protection clause of the Fourteenth Amendment. There were legal technicalities as well, since the statute applied only to those roughly one thousand epileptics, usually the most poor, who lived in state institutions like Skillman. Some worried about another thousand or so epileptics who were free in society. Technicalities aside, Justice Charles Garrison was prescient in his decision, questioning how far things might go if such a law was allowed to stand:

> If the enforced sterility of this class be a legitimate exercise
> of government power, a wide field of legislative activity and
> duty is thrown open to which it would be difficult to assign a
> legal limit.... Racial differences, for instance, might afford a

basis for such an opinion in communities where that question
is unfortunately a permanent and paramount issue.[28]

Harry Laughlin was outraged by this legal setback and vowed
to appeal the Alice Smith decision to New Jersey's Court of Errors
and Appeal, which in those days was higher than the state's Supreme
Court. He threatened that if need be they might pursue the case all
the way to the United States Supreme Court. Laughlin was a zealot
who one year earlier had declared: "To purify the breeding stock of
the race at all costs is the slogan of eugenics.... The mothers of unfit
children should be "relegated to a place comparable to that of the
females of mongrel strains of domestic animals." He complained
that although by then twelve states had enacted laws, only a thousand
people had been sterilized: "A halfway measure will never strike
deeply at the roots of evil."[29]

However, a judicial appeal was not pursued, perhaps because
Justice Garrison also was a member of the higher court. An editorial
in the *Yale Law Journal* fomented that the "mentally defective have
a peculiar bent toward uncontrolled procreation" and warned that if
for cost-savings reasons these individuals were to be released in the
future from state institutions, they would be an unrestrained menace
to society.... uncured and incurable.... once an inmate, always an
inmate."[30] It would be better to "fix them ... while they are under
control, before they are lost in the community." But in his legal
analysis Justice Garrison had anticipated and denounced such an
argument:

> [If] the scheme of the statute were to turn the sterilized
> inmates of such public institutes loose upon the community,
> and thereby to effect a saving of expense to the public, [it
> would not be] deserving of serious consideration. The
> palpable inhumanity and immorality of such a scheme
> forbids us to impute it to an enlightened Legislature that
> evidently enacted the present statute for [what it considered
> to be] a worthy social end.[31]

Judge Charles Garrison wasn't a lone voice against the

potential danger of eugenics, but he was a relatively early critic of what for many had become conventional wisdom. Before deciding to pursue a legal career he had completed medical studies at the University of Pennsylvania and practiced medicine for four years in his hometown, Swedesboro, N.J. Garrison was appointed to the Supreme Court in 1888 and served for thirty-two years, until he retired in 1920. As an admiring colleague recalled him:

[Garrison was a] prodigious reader and a thinker on scientific and philosophical subjects ... a man of great independence [who] quite frequently dissented in opinions that many think are stronger and better grounded than those of the majority. They are as one now reads them. Rather more philosophical than legal. He ranks, I think, among the greatest of our Judges.[32]

Spreading the Word

New Jersey may have been the sixth state to pass an involuntary sterilization law, but it was the first to strike it down on constitutional grounds. Soon several other states followed suit but sterilizations sometimes continued quietly in defiance of the courts. New York's legislature had passed a sterilization law in 1912, and forty-two inmates of state institutions were operated on before in 1918 the Supreme Court, relying on the New Jersey ruling, repealed their law, characterizing it as "inhuman in nature."

Undeterred by the Supreme Court's decision in the Smith case, New Jersey's eugenicists continued to promote their ideology. In February 1913 Superintendent Johnstone hired his brother-in-law, Alexander Johnson, to head Vineland's "Extension Department" which was described as a "publicity and propagandist agency." Alexander Johnson during the 1890s had gained experience in the field working as an administrator at the Indiana School for Feebleminded Youth. E. R. Johnstone and Henry Goddard had initiated the Vineland program in 1910, but demands were overwhelming, not only in New Jersey but far beyond—women's clubs, churches, schools, all were asking for guidance: "Tell us what we can do." At a conference held in New York City in December 1914, New Jersey's Committee on Provision for the Feeble-Minded and Epileptic was recast as a national committee to eradicate feeblemindedness. Joseph P. Byers, formerly

New Jersey's commissioner of charities, was appointed executive director, and Alexander Johnson was appointed field secretary.

Working with Charles Davenport and with financial backing from Mary Harriman, the committee's mission was "To disseminate knowledge concerning the extension and menace of feeblemindedness, and initiate methods for its control and ultimate eradication from the American people." In his initial report, Joseph Byers acknowledged, "never before in any state [as New Jersey] has there been such widespread interest in, and knowledge of, the feeble-minded." The national committee would be based at Vineland, the staff expanded, and the annual budget fixed at $20,000.

Newspapers were preoccupied with World War I so Alexander Johnson went on the lecture circuit speaking to "anyone who would listen." Over the next three years Johnson visited nearly every New Jersey city and town spreading the word about the menace of the feebleminded. He estimated that he spoke to nearly twenty thousand people in 111 lectures in New Jersey alone, and then he took his message on the road, lecturing from Newfoundland to Texas, New Orleans to Illinois. Before long, "the whole country seemed to be becoming feebleminded conscious" and in time he claimed to have given more than eleven hundred lectures. Alexander Johnson explained:

> There was evident need of a wide presentation of the facts, the results of experiment, in a popular, positive, objective way; not merely as it had been done to social workers at national and state conferences; but to the general public. The task was to force upon the attention of the whole people the facts we knew; to convince them of the validity of our methods and of the duty of every state to its feeble-minded; and to induce each to discharge that duty fully.[33]

In 1914 William Graves, president of the American Association for the Study of Epilepsy and the Care and Treatment of Epileptics, reported that although the number of state and private colonies was growing, a national survey estimated that 115,000 epileptics were in need of institutionalization, and there was only a present capacity for seven thousand. Despite New Jersey's Supreme Court decision of the previous year, the subject of mandatory sterilization still was alive, but Dr. Graves remained skeptical:

> Some go so far as to advocate the prevention of procreation by a simple operation on every defective. It is really too early to generally enforce any such laws. Heredity is an only partially explored field and until we make the favorable soil for epilepsy tend to increase or diminish the course of generations, we must not take to drastic measures. To me the solution of all the facts and situations I have recited, lies in the establishment of institutions in which the epileptic can be segregated, spending the remainder of his life in comfort and usefulness.[34]

But Letchworth Village's superintendent, Dr. Charles S. Little, disagreed:

> There is no question but that the lower strata of society is reproducing its kind all out of proportion to the middle and upper classes upon whom we depend for the stability of our government. To meet this situation steps should be taken to protect society before it is overwhelmed by this growing menace. A step in the [right] direction might be made if careful histories were obtained of every inmate of a jail, poorhouse, prison, reformatory and institution for the feeble-minded and if that history should show degenerate and criminalistic antecedents, sterilization should be performed. A beginning at least might be made in lessening the poisonous stream that is undermining the foundation of this government.[35]

Because statutory language was imprecise in some states, in 1922 Harry Laughlin published a model law that would serve as the template for a second wave of eugenic legislation, resulting in eighteen more statutes favoring compulsory sterilization. Laughlin was concerned with the legal issue of denying due process and argued that sterilizations needed to be based on eugenic therapeutic principles rather than performed as punitive measures. Virginia passed a sterilization law in 1924 that was approved by their Supreme Court. However, this decision was appealed to the United States Supreme Court, which included such luminaries as Louis Brandeis and William Howard Taft. The test case of *Buck v. Bell* involved Carrie Buck, a seventeen-year-old resident of a Virginia asylum who had a child out of wedlock. Officials declared her to be feebleminded and promiscuous like her mother, who was institutionalized at the same facility. Expert witnesses argued that Carrie was "a probable potential parent of socially inadequate offspring." In a lower court review the asylum's superintendent, Albert Priddy, had remarked, "The history of all such cases in which mental defectiveness, insanity and epilepsy develop in the generations of feeble-minded persons is that the baneful effects of heredity will be shown in descendents of all future generations."[36]

Harry Laughlin had never met Carrie Buck, but he was pleased to serve as an expert witness favoring sterilization before the United States Supreme Court. Carrie's attorney argued that if the law was permitted to stand, "a reign of doctors will be inaugurated and in the name of science new classes will be added, even races may be brought within the scope of such regulation and the worst form of tyranny practiced." However, Chief Justice Oliver Wendell Holmes, Jr., himself a student of eugenics, ruled that a deficient mother, daughter, and granddaughter justified the need for sterilization. Justice Holmes famously concluded:

> It is better for all the world, if instead of waiting to execute degenerate offspring for crime or to let them starve for their imbecility, society can prevent those who are manifestly unfit from continuing their kind. The principle that sustains compulsory vaccination is broad enough to cover cutting the Fallopian tubes. Three generations of imbeciles are enough.[37]

Five months after the U.S. Supreme Court's decision, Carrie Buck was sterilized. Much later it was found that she hadn't been promiscuous at all but had been raped. Her infant daughter Vivian, whom Holmes had characterized as "a third generation imbecile" grew up to become an honor student in public school, but based on this infamous ruling some eighty-three hundred Virginians eventually were sterilized. The Supreme Court's decision in *Buck v. Bell* unleashed a torrent of new compulsory sterilization laws. During the next ten years statutes were adopted in twenty more states, and despite emerging scientific evidence which refuted the theory that most kinds of mental illness were caused by single gene defects, the number of procedures multiplied.

After *Buck v. Bell* few court challenges were attempted, and those that were addressed involved more the details of laws than the general concept. In time what some people called "Mendelian eugenics" became discredited, and there was a decline of legislative and scientific support. Nevertheless, a review published as late as 1966 noted that at least twenty-three states retained the old laws, and that in more than ten states epileptics and criminals were still considered to be appropriate subjects for sterilization. By the time that the sterilization movement finally ran out of steam during the 1970s, it's likely that more than 65,000 Americans had suffered what one victim described as "sexual murder."[38] Most were performed on poor people, disproportionately blacks, who were confined to state-run institutions for the mentally retarded.

To this day, *Buck v. Bell* has never been overturned.

The Seeds of Hate Are Sown

Charles Davenport, Harry Laughlin, and their eugenicist colleagues pursued their agenda with zeal, with Laughlin testifying in Congress in 1922 on matters relating to immigration and sterilization. Few people argued publicly with them—after all, this was "science," endorsed in high school biology texts and taught at hundreds of American colleges. Before long, application of eugenic ideology would have profound ramifications, including the U.S. Immigration Restriction Act of 1924, which prohibited immigration of those with hereditary illnesses and entire ethnic groups out of concern that America's genetic stock was deteriorating. The law was directed primarily against Eastern and Southern Europeans and predated Nazi immigration laws by more than ten years. In particular, Charles Davenport believed that the influx of Jews posed a threat to his image of the ideal American citizen: the rural Yankee Protestant who lived a temperate, chaste life; Italians and Poles and Negroes also fell outside this ideal.

Henry Goddard may not have been a racist, but his book about the Kallikaks had been translated into German, and in 1933 it was cited as justification for a new German compulsory sterilization law, which will be described presently. One Nazi official observed that the story of the Kallikaks demonstrated how "feeblemindedness ... is the best fecund soil for every form of crime." Some American critics of Henry Goddard's research found his results to be "too good," his data collection sloppy and his conclusions not scientifically valid. It also was suggested that photos of the Kallikak family had been retouched in order to make them appear more moronic. Faced with mounting opposition among Vineland's financial backers, Goddard resigned in 1918 to take a well-paying position at Ohio State University. Ten years later he recanted somewhat, saying that perhaps the risk of hereditary feeblemindedness had been overstated—the moron is not necessarily incurable; the feebleminded do not necessarily need to be segregated, the bar had been set too high: "We have worked too long the old concept ... I think I have gone over to the other camp."[39]

But not entirely. Writing in 1931, Goddard recalled that World War I and the Depression had been catastrophic manifestations of mental defect and grandiosely observed that "the knowledge derived from the testing of 1,700,000 men in the Army is probably the most valuable piece of information which mankind has ever achieved about itself ... There is no longer any doubt about the facts. The little committee of seven which met at the Vineland Laboratory and drafted the Army Mental Tests did a remarkable piece of work, the results of which are destined to be of immeasurable value to the race."[40]

One of that "gang of seven" was Carl C. Brigham, an assistant professor of psychology at Princeton who after working on the Army tests published a book, *A Study of Human Intelligence* (1923), in which he reported that IQ tests proved that the Nordic race was intellectually superior to negroes, Jews, Italians, and other ethnic groups. Based on scientific "facts" derived from the army tests, he argued that immigration should not only be restrictive but highly selective. In 1930 Brigham denounced these views, publicly admitted that the army data were worthless as measures of innate intelligence, and broke with the eugenicists. However, the damage already was done—Brigham's book was influential in convincing Congress to impose harsh quotas against nations of inferior stock. According to historian Stephen Jay Gould, "The eugenicists battled and won one of the greatest victories of scientific racism in American history." Immigration from Europe slowed to a trickle; millions were trapped. As Gould described it, "The paths to destruction are often indirect, but ideas can be agents as sure as guns and bombs."

Carl Brigham had argued for prevention of propagation of defective strains in the population, but whereas most institutional superintendents favored the necessity of segregation, many were publicly silent about forced sterilization. In 1922, faced with growing opposition, Superintendent Johnstone added a young psychiatrist, George Stevenson, to Vineland's research staff, but Stevenson found Goddard's work to be invalid and soon left to join the National Committee on Mental Hygiene, which encouraged mental hygiene and child guidance clinics. Dr. Stevenson's move was typical of a shift of many psychiatrists after the war years toward better understanding of the psychopathology of the feebleminded. As a result, there was no clear consensus among psychiatrists about the wisdom of using an invasive surgical technique on institutionalized patients, especially without their consent. Yet, as interest in heredity was waning, Vineland's Johnstone and Johnson resisted the trend, and with their support new state institutions and schools were opened during the 1920s in Woodbine, New Lisbon, and Totowa. Each of them was intended to address the needs of specific groups of mentally challenged individuals, but as one institutional psychiatrist lamented, "Some better method of preventing human diseases will have to be thought of than human sterilization."

The first generation of eugenicists was departing the scene, but New Jersey's experience with sterilization laws was far from over. During the 1930s and '40s a few zealots persisted. Prominent among them was Marion S. Olden (later known as Marian S. Norton) of Princeton, a social worker and the feminist founder of the League of Women Voters. Intelligent, attractive and opinionated, she was a woman of great tenacity—as she said, "people's feeling don't register with me…. Principles are eternal, human relations may not be." (She married four times.) One of Olden's booklets began with a picture of a mentally handicapped patient and the caption:

See the happy moron;
He doesn't have a care,
His children and his problems
Are all for us to bear. [41]

Like her contemporary Margaret Sanger, Marion Olden was virulently anti-Catholic because of the church's opposition to birth control. In 1934 she became an adherent of the eugenics movement, and, as she saw it, sterilization was the best way to "protect" potential defective beings from being born, as opposed to castration, which she considered to be barbaric. After visiting Vineland and Skillman, she was distressed to learn that some patients were being discharged and "menacing our better stock."[42]

In 1935 Mrs. Olden gathered signatures from physicians and eugenicists, and the League of Women Voters had a sterilization bill introduced in the state Senate. The bill was defeated, but, undaunted, she pursued her crusade. She broke with the League of Women Voters and two years later founded the Sterilization League of New Jersey. In 1938 Mrs. Olden visited Germany, where she was warmly greeted by Nazi eugenicists, who were pleased with her anti-Catholic and racist positions. She was not averse to saying publicly that the United States had become the "dumping ground" for subnormal people from southern and eastern Europe who were congenitally prone to crime and illness. Marian Olden agreed to collaborate with Nazi leaders on a pro-sterilization movie and defended the German sterilization law of 1933 against attacks by the Catholic Church. Other American eugenicists also were proud of their influence on the development of German law, and the official newsletter of the eugenics movement noted that the text of the German statute read almost like Laughlin's model sterilization law: "Its standards are social and genetic. Its application is entrusted to specialized courts and procedures. From a legal point of view, nothing more could be desired." One American eugenicist complained, "The Germans are beating us at our own game."

Even after the outbreak of World War II, the Sterilization League gathered money and influential supporters and in 1942 introduced still another bill to the New Jersey legislature; this time a twenty-four page document titled An Act to Aid the Afflicted by Providing for the Sexual Sterilization of Persons Unfit for Parenthood. It called for a state eugenicist to search all state prisons, hospitals, homes, and asylums in order to find people suffering from mental deficiency or familial epilepsy who were "unable because of such affliction to discharge the responsibilities of parenthood." Parents would be permitted a right of appeal, but the final word would be that of a State Eugenic Council. No legislators dared defy the Catholic Church, and the bill was buried in committee. Mrs. Olden dismissed the church's position as "an obstacle to progress in every form."

Marion Olden's blunt rhetoric antagonized many people and defied evolving societal attitudes; yet, she obstinately held to her belief in sterilization as a form of birth control. After her death in 1970, the league would be influential in framing new ideas. To be sure, the membership became embroiled in bitter power struggles, and the organization changed names several times (in 2001 it became Engender Health.) Its mission expanded beyond New Jersey's borders, and eugenics rhetoric was dropped in favor of promoting "human betterment through voluntary methods." Their political agenda changed to advocate birth control and reproductive rights, and to fight AIDS in third world countries. After World War II, members of the American eugenics movement sought to distance themselves from their former support for Nazi racist policies. The American Eugenics Society morphed to the Society for Study of Social Biology, *Eugenics Quarterly* was retitled *Social Biology*, and Marion Olden's Sterilization League of New Jersey was renamed Birthright. As late as 1976, Mrs. Olden, now eight-eight years old and unrepentant, proudly recalled her support for Nazi race policies.[43] Historian Ian Oldingen remarked, "Olden antagonized friend and foe alike, but in time few doubted that her determination had helped to launch a movement that eventually would change the course of world history."[44]

Men Are Not Created Equal

The eugenic argument in favor of sterilization had been clearly stated back in 1916 by the president of the Eugenics Research Association, Madison Grant, who in his book *The Passing of the Great Race* declared that the idea of the United States as a "melting pot is an absolute failure."

> The individual himself can be nourished, educated, and protected by the community during his lifetime, but the state through sterilization must see to it that his line stops with him, or else future generations will be cursed with an ever increasing load of victims of misguided sentimentalism. This is a practical, merciful and inevitable solution of the whole problem, and can be applied to an ever widening circle of social discards beginning always with the criminal, the diseased, and the insane, and extending gradually to types which may be called weaklings rather than defectives and perhaps ultimately to worthless race types.[45]

Perhaps the most outspoken and influential spokesman for aggressive eugenics policy during the 1920s and 1930s was the Nobel Prize winning surgeon Alexis Carrel of the Rockefeller Institute.[46] In an interview with the *New York Times* he declared, "There is no escaping the fact that men are not created equal ... the fallacy of equality … was invented in the eighteenth century when there was no science to correct it." Dr. Carrel held that society must identify and encourage those with greatest ability, while the dregs should be "disposed of in small euthanistic institutions supplied with the proper gases[!].… Why preserve useless and harmful beings?" The work of creating useful and beneficial beings should be directed by a "high council of experts" living in seclusion like monks—"audacious men of science, unafraid of resorting to extreme, even ruthless measures." He added that "man cannot remake himself without suffering for he is both marble and sculptor. In order to recover his true visage, man must shatter his own substance with heavy blows of the hammer." In 1936 Dr. Carrel elaborated his social prescriptions in *Man, the Unknown*, which was the year's top-selling nonfiction book, second overall only to the novel *Gone with the Wind*. That same year, the famous surgeon's face appeared on the cover of *Time* magazine in company with the likes of Benito Mussolini, Douglas MacArthur, and J. Edgar Hoover.

Alexis Carrel was not alone among American physicians to publicly advocate euthanasia as a more definitive solution than sterilization. When a severely deformed baby was born in Chicago in 1915, the hospital's medical director had convinced the mother not to treat the child, but to let it die. The doctor revealed that he had let a number of "defectives" die in the past and would continue to do so. This case was widely reported by the newspapers, and the decision was publicly supported by such well-known figures as Clarence Darrow and Helen Keller. Subsequently the case was enacted in a movie, *The Black Stork*, which was widely distributed and discussed for many years. The issue lingered, and a Gallup poll in 1937 reported that 45 percent of Americans favored euthanasia for defective infants.

In 1936 a report was issued by a special committee of the American Neurological Association that had been charged with investigating the issue of eugenical sterilization. Experiences in several states were reviewed, and it was concluded that even when statutes permitting compulsory sterilization existed, relatively few procedures were being performed. The committee noted that contrary to fears by eugenicists, mental disease did not appear to be increasing, and although there were concerns that the feebleminded can be a financial drain on society, "being servile [they can be] useful people who do the dirty work of the race." They concluded that although sufficient valid research was lacking, most of the legislation which had been enacted so far had been based upon a desire to elevate the human race. Voluntary sterilization was recommended for several categories, including hereditary neurological diseases, "familial feeble-mindedness," schizophrenia, manic-depressive psychosis, and epilepsy.

Physicians Andre Sofair and Lauris Kaldjian recently reviewed editorials on the subject of eugenic sterilization that had appeared in the pages of the influential *New England Journal of Medicine* and *Journal of the American Medical Association* and other journals between 1930 and 1936. Presumably, these reflected prevalent attitudes in the medical profession.[47] The *NEJM* editors were especially concerned with the financial and public health dangers posed by "mentally defective classes," and in response to Germany's newly enacted compulsory sterilization law, in 1934 a *NEJM* editorial described Germany as "perhaps the most progressive nation in restricting fecundity among the unfit." They argued that "the individual must give way before the greater good" but recognized that "until public sentiment [in the United States] can be molded to look at the matter in a scientific spirit, it will be necessary to employ moral suasion in getting the largest number of assents to advice for the application of this treatment." The editors of *JAMA* were more circumspect:

> In Germany, mass sterilization is presumably being carried out. A more gradual evolution of the practice and principles has occurred in this country. Judging from the uncertain biologic foundation on which human sterilization rests, the latter would seem a less dangerous procedure. While recognizing the possible potential value of sterilization, the medical profession can perhaps serve its purpose best by retaining a scientific detachment in assessing the biological and social results of the programs now in force.[49]

It wasn't until 1936 that more skeptical medical writers began putting Nazi takeover of science into perspective, describing it as "strangulation of intellectualism" and started placing quotation marks around Nazi medical expressions and statements to differentiate them from ordinary medical discourse.

For the Good of the State

So far, I've only briefly alluded to events in Germany during the 1930s, but now it is necessary to consider them in greater detail, for if the United States led the way in developing and implementing eugenic theory, it was in Germany that the evil outcome of these ideas came to fruition. Indeed, concerns about the quality of the hereditary stock in Germany had been voiced as early as the 1890s, long before the advent of National Socialism. There was a sense that Darwinian natural selection could not be trusted, and in order to avert racial deterioration proactive measures were called for. In 1905 a Racial Hygiene Society was founded in Berlin, and its members generally assumed a genetic superiority of "Aryans" over other races. By the end of World War I, "race hygiene," as eugenics was called, gained broad acceptance within academic, professional, and even some religious circles. There were concerns about the recent loss of good-stock Aryan lives as well as disastrous inflation and national humiliation over the terms of the Versailles Treaty which had ended the war. What began as an abstract debate over principles of social Darwinism became politicized, and within this context sterilization of the mentally and physically "inferior" appeared to be a logical biological solution to social and economic problems. The prevailing view was that society was a living organism, the *Volk*, with its own health, and individuals were valued either as functional or dysfunctional parts of this greater whole. Now into this witch's brew came American eugenicists, whose example legitimated the theory. However, it took a dictator to implement the radical ideas and steer them in a catastrophic new direction.

German eugenicists admired how American emigration policies enacted during the 1920s permitted only "the fittest" to enter and returned Jewish "inferiors" to their ports of origin. One scholar urged Germans to catch up with the Americans, who had become the acknowledged world leader in racial hygiene. In 1936 Harry Laughlin was awarded an honorary degree by the University of Heidelberg for his work in the science of "racial cleansing." The diploma lauded him as a "successful pioneer of practical eugenics and the farseeing representative of racial policy in America." Laughlin understood this as "evidence of a common understanding of German and American scientists of the nature of eugenics." Although he did not travel to Germany to personally accept the award, he was proud of the "high honor."[49]   (Ironically, in his later years Laughlin developed uncontrolled seizures. Although he and his family tried to keep this secret, Laughlin had several witnessed convulsions, so the man who would sterilize all epileptics would have been eligible for the same procedure he advocated for others.)

Eugenic sterilization laws passed in Denmark (1929), Sweden and Norway (1934), Finland (1935), Estonia (1937), Iceland (1938) and barely failed to pass in England and the Netherlands.[50] Voluntary sterilization bills had been introduced in Prussia as early as 1903 and discussed before the Reichstag in 1907 and 1925. Adolf Hitler was impressed by the work of Professor Ernst Ruden of the University of Munich, who was a leading proponent of sterilization as being the most efficient and humane way of ridding society of "bad heredity." Hitler also had read translations of the books of Charles Davenport, Madison Grant, and Henry Goddard while in prison in 1923–24 and was familiar with American sterilization laws. In *Mein Kampf* Hitler wrote that "as a result of our modern 'sentimental' humanitarianism, we are trying to maintain the weak at the expense of the healthy." The right to personal freedom would have to give way to the duty of preserving "the master race." For the good of the state it was necessary to ensure that "those unfit to live" would not propagate. This message appealed to people both on the political left and the right. Who could argue with giving careful thought to marriage partners or preserving family values or leading a temperate lifestyle? Serious scientists, scholars, and jurists accepted that at stake was preservation of the human species, and the economic argument was powerful—caring for the chronically ill had become an unaffordable luxury.

Dr. Karl Bonhoeffer, chairman of the German Psychiatry Association, explained, "It could almost seem as if we have witnessed a change in the concept of humanity." A Protestant leader described "a moral duty which can be explained as a love of one's neighbor and responsibility towards future generations."[51]   Concerned about sanctity of life, most Catholic leaders were unenthusiastic but failed to publicly criticize laws which prohibited marriage or sexual relations between Jews and non-Jews, between "diseased" and "healthy" races. Hitler ranted that the role of the strongest is to dominate and not to melt in with the weakest. Propaganda Minister Joseph Goebbels was even more blunt: "Our starting point is not the individual and we do not subscribe to the view that one should feed the hungry, give drink to the thirsty or clothe the naked … our objectives are entirely different; we must have a healthy people in order to prevail in the world."

Nazi Sterilization

The tragic evolution from eugenics theory to sterilization policy and then to euthanasia and genocide officially began on January 30, 1933, when Hitler was appointed chancellor. Within months the Nazis consolidated their power, and laws were enacted to isolate, exclude, and eventually eliminate the unwanted. An Act for the Prevention of Genetically Diseased Offspring passed with little opposition on July 14, 1933, which was based on racial purity and national health. Since racial hygiene linked the handicapped to criminal and antisocial behavior, laws intended to eradicate "inherited criminal traits" seemed perfectly reasonable to many German citizens. Those religious leaders who were informed of the government's plans voiced no major opposition, and most medical and academic leaders were enthusiastic supporters.

The first to be singled out were approximately five hundred young offspring of German women and colonial African soldiers, who were referred to as "Rhineland Bastards."[52] Hitler attributed this miscegenation as a method that was devised by Jews in order to pollute German blood, and sterilization offered a solution. Next a registry of medically unfit inmates of German asylums was developed, and doctors and hospital administrators were required to provide medical records of all of their patients, which were reviewed by so-called "racial biology" specialists. At first sterilization was voluntary—meaning that doctors and nurses "encouraged" patients or their families to agree for their own good. More than two hundred Health Courts were set up to consider each case and to give an aura of due process, but medical review was cursory. What began as voluntary soon became compulsory, at least for certain illnesses, and the qualifier of there being hereditary disorders was dropped so that all manner of physical and mental conditions would be eligible. Of some eighty-five thousand cases reviewed by the Hereditary Health Courts in 1934-1936 about 90 percent were approved for sterilization. Although there was a right of appeal, only about three percent of appealed decisions were reversed. Those who refused to submit to sterilization generally were sent to concentration camps. During the first year of the program 32,268 sterilizations were performed, 53 percent because of congenital mental deficiency, (which included intelligence defect, "lack of life justification" and "poor social adaptability") 25 percent for schizophrenia, and 14 percent for epilepsy. Feeblemindedness was based on an oral test of "acquired knowledge" which was scored subjectively.[53]

In all, nearly four hundred thousand German people, about 1 percent of the population, were sterilized—an average of more than fifty thousand per year before the onset of war. The program continued during the war years at a much reduced rate—only about 5 percent of all sterilizations being performed between 1939 and 1945. Most of those who received the so-called "Hitler-cut" were between the ages of twenty and forty. The usual method was vasectomy for men, tubal ligation for women. Approximately two thousand people died of complications, mostly women because of the more invasive surgery. Victims weren't always aware of what was happening. Sometimes men would be seated in special chairs, and while filling out paperwork, unknowingly, X-rays were directed at their genitals— after a few minutes the damage was done. During the 1920s many physicians had resisted the move toward involuntary sterilization. Implementing the new law required medical cooperation, and Hitler appealed directly to the profession: "I could, if need be, do without lawyers, engineers and builders, but you National Socialist doctors, I cannot do without you for a single day, not a single hour. If you fail me, then all is lost. For what good are our struggles, if the health of our people is in danger."

By 1933 the German medical profession succumbed to propaganda and became "executives of the eugenic will of the nation." Anti-Semitism was "medicalized," as doctors were among the earliest and most active participants in the Nazi movement (about half of German physicians were members of the Nazi party, far more than with any other profession.) Medical journals published articles supporting racist ideology, and for many physicians there were pragmatic benefits as well. Participating in the government programs provided new career opportunities as well as state funding for research projects of the right kind. It was not merely a few bad apples who cooperated but the mainstream medical establishment itself. The German Medical Association perpetrated the idea that Jews suffered from certain hereditary diseases and warned against the dangers of intermarriage. Because Nazi rhetoric described Jews as being "a diseased race," it seemed appropriate to rid the nation of its biologic problem by medical means. Racist ideology was bureaucratized, faceless, sanctioned by the professional leadership, and there was a "herd effect"—others were doing it; they were following orders; they were not responsible.

Down the Slippery Slope

In 1939 the sterilization program was replaced by what euphemistically was called "mercy killing."

The idea of destroying "useless idiots" had been discussed before but wasn't initiated on a grand scale until 1939, which the German government designated as the year of "the duty to be healthy." Whereas during the period from 1933 to 1939 nearly four hundred thousand Germans had been sterilized, during the next six years more than two hundred thousand citizens were euthanized. These included many of the "superfluous" who previously had been sterilized. For those with "substantial mental infirmity," the most important criterion was their ability to work. Patients confined to mental institutions were killed because it was cheaper than caring for them.[53]

The Nazi euthanasia program was given the code name "Aktion T4" because the address of the secret administrative headquarters was No. 4 Tiergartenstrasse. Initially Jewish children were excluded from the operation on the grounds that they did not deserve this "merciful act." Beginning in 1940, the list of eligible gradually expanded to include Jews, gypsies, homosexuals, the chronically ill, the old, the indigent—the different. No marginalized group was safe from Nazi "mercy." Those deemed unworthy to live had to be weeded out. In early 1941 the Reich Ministry of the Interior ordered that all Jews in German hospitals be killed—not because they met the criteria required for euthanasia, but because they were Jews.

There is an important distinction between how we use the word euthanasia today and what it meant to the Nazis. The dictionary definition is of a quiet or easy death, and nowadays the concept emphasizes an individual's legal and moral right to choose life or death for themselves. In contrast, the Nazi approach emphasized the state's right to kill for its own sake. Hitler described his motives as "humanitarian," and although he'd had these murderous ideas much earlier when he was in prison writing *Mein Kampf,* he knew they would not be universally well-received unless he could implement them under the pretext of war. Therefore, in order to provide legal cover, his order to initiate the T4 program was backdated to September 1, 1939—the same day that war broke out.

When the T4 operation began it was limited to deformed infants, microcephalics, congenital heart cases, and the like who were below age three. Soon the age threshold rose to eight, then to twelve, then sixteen. Parents were given misinformation; if they dared to protest, they were threatened with reprisals. During this first phase about five thousand children were killed by starvation or exposure or poisoning. But the genie was out of the bottle; the healers had become killers, and the search widened for new victims and methods. Within a few months the rules changed again. Now the target was adult patients with psychiatric disorders. Physicians at state asylums were told that it was necessary to kill a proportion of patients in order to create bed space for anticipated war wounded. Doctors were recruited with offers of double pay and special privileges, or exemption from being sent to the front lines. Many declined; others signed on—why not? After all, everyone seemed to agree that these people were "useless eaters."

In 1939 the German military took over a small mental asylum in the town of Hadamar, and within a few months certain unusual structural changes were made.[54] A special shower room was installed in the basement together with a crematorium with two ovens. Beginning in January 1941, large grey buses with their windows painted over began arriving like clockwork each day carrying patients from nearby mental asylums. Signs on the road leading to Hadamar warned of the danger of epidemics and prohibited entry, but the local citizens could tell by the smell of the pervasive chimney smoke what was going on. Between January and August 1941, an average of one hundred people were killed every day. They were brought directly to the shower room and stripped; the doors were closed, air was sucked out, and for about ten minutes carbon monoxide was pumped in. The whole process usually took about an hour. Gold was extracted from teeth, and a few fresh bodies were saved for medical experimentation; then the corpses were brought directly to the ovens. A checklist of sixty suitable causes of death was distributed for the doctor's convenience when falsifying death certificates. Families were sent sympathetic letters such as, "your son died of blood poisoning from warts on his lips." Hadamar was only the last of six killing centers that were opened for the T4 operation, but between January and August 1941, 10,072 people were gassed there. After the ten thousand mark was passed, a macabre celebratory staff party was held, with beer served to all.

Resistance to Euthanasia

Nazi propaganda was effective, and the euthanasia program received broad public support. Some parents of handicapped children even requested the procedure. Similarly, when the program expanded to include mentally ill adults, elimination of these unwanted people seemed to be logical, even humane. A few brave people objected, but the Gestapo was relentless, and the T4 operation continued uninterrupted for about two years. The Vatican had signed a Concordat in July 1933 in which they agreed to refrain from becoming involved in politics, and their reaction to the sterilization laws was token or ambiguous. Concerning the euthanasia program, it took about six months, until the full extent of the T4 program was undeniable, before church authorities officially began to react. The charismatic Catholic leader Bishop Clement von Galen protested privately to the authorities, but when his pleas were ignored, on August 3, 1941, he delivered a sermon criticizing the euthanasia program:

> Have you, have I, the right to live only so long as we are recognized by others as being productive?....If this dreadful doctrine is tolerated, accepted and followed.... Woe to mankind, woe to our German nation if God's Holy Commandment "Thou shalt not kill" is not only broken but

if this transgression is actually tolerated and permitted to go unpunished.[55]

Bishop Galen sent a copy of his sermon directly to Hitler, calling upon him to defend the people against the Gestapo: "We are talking about men and women, our compatriots, our brothers and sisters. Poor unproductive people if you wish, but does this mean that they have lost the right to live?" Galen gave three public sermons, which, although unreported in the German press, were widely circulated as illegally printed leaflets. Some Nazi leaders wanted to hang the bishop for his insolence, but Hitler and Goebels realized that this might spark a revolt and chose to ignore him. In fact, there was a public outcry which was unique during the Nazi era, and three weeks later Hitler ordered the euthanasia program to be suspended—at least officially. Bishop Galen and a very few others who disagreed with the T4 operation were speaking only for their own flocks, and their public statements did not extend to the Jews or other targeted groups. An exception was Bernhard Lichtenberg, provost of a Catholic church in Berlin, who in his condemnation of euthanasia specifically criticized Nazi persecution of the Jews. For his trouble, Lichtenberg was committed to a concentration camp and killed on his way to Dachau.

Bishop Galen's message influenced a group of idealistic students at the University of Munich, who were pleased that at last someone had spoken up. They organized a covert organization which called for passive resistance against the regime, and, for reasons that still are unclear, they used the code name "The White Rose"—perhaps to symbolize their purity of spirit. Among the leaders were twenty-one-year-old Sophie Scholl and her older brother Hans, who was a medical student. Hans and some friends had been conscripted into the army as medics and while on the eastern front saw naked Jews being machine-gunned in an open pit. The Scholls and a small group of students called for others to rise up, and for eight months, using a small copying machine, they secretly published six pamphlets that were distributed widely throughout Germany. The group's rallying cry was, "We will not be silent. We are your bad conscience. The White Rose will not leave you in peace." Because of his reputation,

Bishop Galen escaped punishment and survived the war—shortly before his death in 1946 he was elevated to cardinal. Sophie and Fritz Scholl were beheaded. Later some pamphlets reached England, and the RAF dropped millions of copies over Germany retitled "The Manifesto of the Students of Munich."

Although the T4 operation was officially suspended because of the public outcry sparked by Bishop Galen, that didn't end the program—it only changed the methodology. To be sure, the installations in the cellar at Hadamar were converted back to sickrooms, but soon a second stage began, which was referred to as "wild" euthanasia; killings continued but less systematically. Now doctors were encouraged to devise their own methods, and they usually reverted to what had worked best in the past—injecting lethal doses of barbiturates or narcotics, or "natural" death by deliberate starvation. Pseudodiagnoses written on death certificates often cited "tuberculosis" although there was no objective evidence of that disease.

Even after the onset of World War II, American eugenicists continued to visit Germany. In the winter of 1939–1940 geneticist Tage Ellinger visited colleagues at the Kaiser Wilhelm Institute and was impressed by the "amazing amount of unbiased information" being collected there, particularly how it "could play an important role in defining whether or not a person had Jewish ancestors." After his return to the United States, Ellinger described his findings in the American Genetic Association's *Journal of Heredity*:

> In itself, the problem [of the Jews] is a fairly simple one when it is understood that the deliberate eradication of the Jewish element in Germany has nothing whatever to do with religious persecution. It is entirely a large-scale breeding project, with the purpose of eliminating from the nation the hereditary attributes of the Semitic race. Whether this is desirable or not is a question that has nothing to do with science. It is a matter of policy and prejudice only. It is a problem similar to that [which] Americans have solved to their own satisfaction with regard to the colored population ... Genetics really seems to have an unlimited field of practical applications, but I am sure that the old priest Mendel would have had the

shock of his life had he been told that seventy-five years after he planted his unpretentious peas in the monastery garden of Brunn, his new science would be called upon to "grade up" the "scrub" population of Germany to new "standards of Aryan perfection."[56]

After *Kristallnacht*—the "night of broken glass" in November 1938 when hundreds of German synagogues were destroyed, tens of thousands of stores were ransacked, ninety Jews were murdered and more than thirty thousand were arrested—there was no more pretense. What had begun as a public health measure inexorably transformed into targeted genocide against one segment of the population. Government policy based on maintaining racial purity, and seemingly cost-efficient too, was embraced by German society. All of Europe would be made *Judenrein*— free of Jews. The first million or so civilians killed in Europe at the beginning of the war died as a result of face-to-face shootings or beatings, but many SS soldiers were emotionally traumatized by their actions—what today would be called "posttraumatic stress disorder." However, the gassing technique that had been perfected in the euthanasia program impressed the leaders—it wasn't one on one and was far more efficient. And if gas no longer was suitable to use on German soil, it could be particularly helpful in the newly occupied territories, where the problem was what to do with millions of prisoners in concentration camps. About one hundred former T4 doctors were sent to the East to bring their expertise to killing camps like Auschwitz, where doctors wore SS uniforms, and the actual killers wore white coats and stethoscopes in a cynical perversion of medical routine. Carbon monoxide was replaced by Zyklon gas, a faster, cyanide-based insecticide. At his Nuremberg trial after the war, Dr. Karl Brandt proudly told his interrogators that the technique of mass killing by gas represented an important medical advance.

Bethel: The House of God

The founders of Skillman Village had been inspired by the *von Bodelschwingenschen Anstalten* "epileptic colony" located in Bielefeld, in the province of Westphalia, and better known as the Bethel Institute—the name being derived from the Hebrew word for "House of God." Opened in 1867, the asylum had developed an outstanding reputation as an integrated and harmonious Christian community. The founding fathers of both Bethel and Skillman were succeeded by their sons, respectively David Weeks at Skillman in 1907 and Friedrich von Bodelschwingh ("Pastor Fritz") at Bethel in 1910. Perhaps the sons met in 1912 when Dr. Weeks, as newly elected president of the International League Against Epilepsy, visited Bethel and reported back to his board at Skillman, "The spirit of brotherly love is ... fully developed here [at Bethel]—nowhere have I seen such devotion of employees and patients for each other as at this Colony. Each seems to be vying with the other to see who can be most kind and polite."[57]

Both Skillman's and Bethel's leaders approved of eugenic sterilization as a means of dealing with the problems of certain groups of the mentally handicapped. American supporters of Bethel mailed Pastor Fritz information about the progress of eugenics in the United States, and during the 1920s he and other Protestant clergymen were actively calling for sterilization laws: "Those who are hereditary carriers of social inferiority and needing care should be excluded from procreating if possible." In 1931, two years before the National Socialist regime enacted its sterilization law, Pastor Fritz, speaking at the Protestant Specialist Conference on Eugenics, explained, "I would be apprehensive if sterilizations were only accepted in cases of emergency. I would prefer to see these procedures as a responsibility conforming to the will of Christ." He spoke of his "deep reverence" for research in this area, for in his view the physically and mentally impaired were "God's abomination to man and reminders ... of the connection between guilt and atonement."[58]

Bethel's medical director from 1930–1933, Carl Schneider was a much admired psychiatrist who reputedly was empathetic to his epileptic patients. Apparently he had a change of heart, joined the Nazi movement, and, as one colleague described, transformed from "a modest scholar with an umbrella and briefcase occupied with the most subtle kind of investigation of schizophrenia ... to a man who as a leader of German psychiatry took on the mission of preaching National Socialism."[61] Himself a pastor's son, Dr. Schneider declared that religious concerns should not stand in the way of the "new ideology." He left Bethel in 1934 to become chairman of psychiatry and neurology in Heidelberg, where he supported government policies and later performed "medical research" on the brains of euthanized victims.[59]

In 1934, the first year of the official German program, 1,219 inmates of state mental facilities in Westphalia were sterilized—about 13 percent of all institutionalized patients. Between 1934 and 1945 more than one thousand Bethel inmates were sterilized, and these procedures continued there at least into the 1970s. At first there was uncertainty about whether or to what degree efforts should be made to obtain consent, but as time went on distinctions blurred between voluntariness and compulsion. In 1962 Pastor Fritz's nephew, who had succeeded his uncle as head of the institution, after reviewing old files concluded that at Bethel the sterilization act had been practiced "diligently ... with no fundamental protest ... based on Christian belief."

By the 1930s Bethel was a small town that housed more than eight thousand patients—about a quarter of them epileptics—in a complex of nursing homes, hospitals, and clinics. At the onset of the T4 euthanasia program in 1939, questionnaires about patients' medical records were sent to all asylums and chronic hospitals and had to be completed and returned within one month. Pastor Fritz, realizing that it would be a death sentence for thousands of his flock, now, finally, objected. Apparently he believed that it would be more effective to work against the euthanasia program behind the scenes and not speak publicly. He had been alerted about the scale of the program by Pastor Paul Braune, who headed an asylum in Berlin, and the two theologians joined in appealing to government officials. Because they were not permitted to speak directly to Hitler, Pastor Fritz wrote to Herman Goering, whose brother-in-law was a patient at Bethel, objecting to "economic planning" measures. The reply was that he had been badly misinformed about the program. Historians differ about how actively Pastor Fritz resisted. In an attempt to delay, apparently he told officials that he did not wish to be difficult, but that his own staff would not do the paperwork. However, he would not stand in the way if state representatives reviewed medical records and completed the questionnaires themselves. Finally, he was given the opportunity to discuss the program directly with Hitler's own physician, Dr. Karl Brandt, who headed the T4 operation, and Brandt was impressed with the theologian's passionate objections. Pastor Fritz pointed out that Bethel was a functional community in which patients were productive citizens. In a letter dated August 28, 1941, Pastor Fritz wrote for a last time to Karl Brandt:

> In the great spiritual struggle now going on, all depend upon the face which the German State displays to the world. Many people see an alarming sign of unrestrained brutality in the State's secretive and unwarranted intervention into the vital circle of family life. …We are giving our enemies weapons against us. A measure that may have been born out of a convinced racist idealism is leading to more and more hate between countries and to a prolongation of the war. The world's History is also the world's Court. That is why I'm fearful that many German mothers will have to pay for the crime charged against our country with nothing less than the blood of their sons.[60]

To what extent Karl Brandt heeded Pastor Fritz's appeal to exempt Bethel's patients from euthanasia is unclear because within a few weeks the entire T4 operation was suspended by Hitler—the original goal of seventy thousand victims already had been reached. Apparently Pastor Fritz believed that his appeal to Brandt had been successful, and shortly after the war's end, on a BBC radio broadcast in 1945, he commented, "You must not picture Professor Brandt as a criminal but rather as an idealist." He felt that Brandt had been willing to listen and was not motivated by brutality. Pastor Fritz died in January 1946 and was succeeded at Bethel by his nephew, who asked that Karl Brandt be pardoned. At the Nuremberg Doctor's Trial pardon was denied, and the mastermind of T4 was hanged in 1948.[61]

Today, while Skillman Village is a nearly forgotten footnote to history, Bethel thrives. From its beginning its leaders were effective fund-raisers, and the Bethel Institute is the largest Protestant charity in Europe, with six related facilities whose combined staffs exceed fourteen thousand workers. They care for many thousands of people who suffer from various chronic mental and physical ailments and are supported by over three hundred and fifty thousand financial contributors. Praiseworthy as this is, there still are a few left who remember events during the 1930s and tell a different story. At an international conference in Dresden, Germany, in June 2007, sponsored by the World Psychiatric Organization, a ninety–year-old former Bethel inmate, Dorothea Buck, delivered the keynote speech, "70 Years of Coercion in German Psychiatric Institutions, Experienced and Witnessed." Describing herself as an "historical witness," Dorothea Buck recalled:

In 1936, 71 years ago—at the age of just 19, I went through the most inhuman experience of my life in a psychiatric institution, against which even being buried alive during the 2nd World War paled into insignificance. I experienced the psychiatric system as being so inhuman because nobody spoke with us. A person cannot be more devalued than to be considered unworthy or incapable of conversation. What made it worse was the fact that this happened at the "von

Bodelschwinghsche Asylum Bethel" in Bielefeld which considered itself a "Christian" institution. Bethel and its director, Pastor Fritz von Bodelschwingh were held in high esteem, thought of as an embodiment of compassion in my parent's home.... But now I got to experience a totally different Bethel, compared to the one I had learned about from the newsletter "Messenger from Bethel."[62]

Dorothea Buck, who suffered from periods of schizophrenia in her early years, described how she was forced to endure being wrapped in cold wet sheets for twenty-three hours at a time:

> I would cry out in rage at this senseless restraint ... I just couldn't believe that the natural way of helping in the form of conversation and occupation was being replaced by these torturous "sedative measures." It was only natural that we got restless without occupation and diversion, without a single conversation, not even as part of the admission procedure and staying in bed all the time, despite being in good health physically. How were we to recognize this senseless kind of behavior on the part of the doctors and nurses as "helping" us?

Like all of the other young women on her ward, Dorothea Buck was subjected to an "appendectomy," learning only after the fact from another patient the true nature of her operation. In all, she was institutionalized five times between 1936 and 1959 but eventually made a full recovery and became a passionate critic of conventional psychiatric care. Because she was stigmatized as being "inferior," Dorothea had to abandon her chosen profession as a kindergarten teacher. In later years she became a prolific writer and lecturer and eventually understood the extent of Nazi perversions of medical science and how later politicians, psychiatrists, and theologians had suppressed the events of the 1930s and 1940s. The ninety-year-old "historical witness" declared, "It is up to us users and survivors of psychiatry to preserve the memory of those murdered in the name of psychiatry in our hearts." Dorothea Buck concluded her polemic against psychiatrists with these words:

How can we trust a psychiatric system that rejects the concept of healing, because it contradicts the theory of the senseless, incurable metabolic brain disorder? We, older people, who have experienced psychosis have paid for this genetic-somatic dogma with forced sterilization and the consequences thereof, and the "euthanasia" victims paid for it with their lives. Now is the time for the psychiatric system to become an empirical science based on the experiences of patients.

Decline of the Villages

During World War I and the years immediately afterward Skillman Village fell on hard times. Many of the staff left to serve in the army, state funds diminished, and the influenza pandemic of 1918 affected half of the inmates, with sixty-five dying. David Weeks served as superintendent throughout this difficult period until his death in 1929. In 1938 Skillman's inmates were among the first to be given the experimental drug Dilantin. With the subsequent widespread availability of anticonvulsants, and then during the 1950s with the emergence of effective antipsychotic drugs, segregated institutions for epileptics and the mentally ill gradually became obsolete. In 1953, 60 percent of Skillman's residents were discharged to other programs, and the facility's mission was expanded to include additional categories of patients. Its name was changed in 1953 to the New Jersey Neuro-Psychiatric Institute and later to the North Princeton Development Center, but as physical conditions deteriorated the former "lunatic asylum" now sometimes was referred to as "the snake pit of New Jersey."

In 1956 a State Commission on Mental Health was established, which surveyed all the ramifications of the problems of the mentally challenged in New Jersey. Its report in 1961 showed a deep concern for these unfortunates and recommended consolidation of existing statutes and reform of administrative policies. The commission recommended that facilities be readily available for all who needed them and that the primary emphasis should be on rehabilitation. Procedures for voluntary entrance and withdrawal from mental hospitals were advised as well as greater availability of outpatient services.

In 1950 novelist Pearl S. Buck, who already had won Pulitzer and Nobel prizes for her novel *The Good Earth*, published an article in *Ladies Home Journal* called "The Child Who Never Grew."[63] In it she told the story of her mentally impaired daughter Carol, who in 1929 at age nine was admitted to Vineland. Pearl Buck wanted Carol to be in a safe environment with "her own kind" and although initially reluctant to institutionalize her daughter was impressed by Superintendent Johnstone's warmth and the school's motto, "Happiness first and all else follows." Mrs. Buck downplayed the importance of heredity in mental illness (it later was discovered that Carol suffered from phenylketonuria), and she was financially generous to Vineland, which she considered to be the finest facility of its kind in the country. By telling Carol's story, a secret that she had not revealed for twenty-five years, Pearl Buck brought public awareness to a subject which previously was taboo. Soon there were more personal testimonies by prominent parents of retarded children, especially the cowboy movie stars Roy Rogers and Dale Evans, and gradually as a result of this increased attention the institutional model of care shifted in favor of community-based mental health services. Carol Buck lived at Vineland from 1929 until her death at age seventy-two in 1992, only a few years before the last residents were discharged.

Henry Goddard lived to age ninety, but always remained perplexed by the fact that later generations found his studies done at Vineland to be dangerous to society. As late as 1943 he still was vigorously defending the methodology that he had employed three decades earlier. He explained that he hadn't intended his Kallikak book to prove Anglo-Saxon superiority, but he did share common stereotypes of his day, including that Jews were cheap or smart. Such ideas were not included in his published works, but he did occasionally use metaphors which compared the feebleminded to mosquitoes or other pests, and these were seized upon by the Nazis to justify their own rhetoric. Speaking in 1948 at the fortieth anniversary of Letchworth Village, the aging prophet remarked:

> The old idea of custodial care for a group of animal-like human beings herded in barracks, half-fed and with a minimum of care is gone forever. Instead, we have here [at Letchworth, as at Vineland] a well-regulated home for 4,000 humans who would otherwise be compelled to live as outcasts, more scorned than pitied."[64]

But Goddard's assessment didn't accurately match facts on the ground. When Letchworth Village Home for the Feeble Minded and Epileptic opened near Haverstraw, New York, in 1911 it had been lauded as a model facility. Planned by one of the country's leading landscape architects, the buildings had Greek porticos and columns and the bucolic two thousand acre campus was within sight of the Hudson River. Superintendent Charles Little described Letchworth as "a home, a school and a laboratory," and its influential sponsors included Charles Davenport, E. R. Johnstone, and the ever financially supportive Mary Harriman. In 1932 Mrs. Harriman arranged for the famous photographer Margaret Bourke White to do a series of photographs which idealized Letchworth Village. However, as time passed there was overcrowding and understaffing; naked residents and filth were ubiquitous, and later photographers recorded grim and grimy scenes. This decline culminated in 1972 in a devastating television series by investigative reporter Geraldo Rivera. Focusing on Willowbrook State Hospital on Staten Island and Letchworth Village, Rivera characterized conditions at these model facilities as "the last great disgrace."[65]

Even as objections to eugenic sterilization began to gain the upper hand, sterilizations continued, and between 1935 and 1956 thirty-eight thousand more procedures were performed. In 1942 the United States Supreme Court again considered a compulsory sterilization law, this time a statute from Oklahoma. By then some of the justices were more sensitive than their predecessors, with William O. Douglas observing, "The power to sterilize if exercised may have subtle, far reaching and devastating effects." In 1977 New Jersey's legislature outlawed sterilization of any developmentally disabled people without the express and informed consent of the individual or his or her guardian. Three years later New Jersey's Supreme Court overruled this in the case of Lee Ann Grady, a nineteen-year-old woman with Down syndrome, whose parents asked their physician to have her sterilized. Morristown Memorial Hospital refused unless the Gradys obtained court permission, and on February 18, 1981, the state's Supreme Court ruled that courts, not parents, should decide whether sterilization of mentally incompetent patients would be permissible, establishing strict guidelines that should frame any such judicial review.[66]

Today on the pastoral campus of Skillman Village boarded-up, dilapidated buildings bear mute testimony to an earlier time. But about the scene of decay hovers a dark shadow which recalls misguided policies that once were pursued there. Skillman's last residents were discharged in 1998, just one hundred years after the first had arrived, and most of the land has been sold off. However, the last 250 acres became a contentious issue between Montgomery Township and the state, with concerns about environmental safety and spiraling demolition costs delaying final resolution. So the final chapter of Skillman's history remains incomplete. As for the other colonies and villages described here, Geraldo Rivera's television series may have been the last straw. Henry Goddard would not recognize the Vineland Training School of today. It was taken over in 1981 by Elwyn Institutes of Media, Pennsylvania, which in 1997 placed all of the residents in small group homes located throughout southern New Jersey. That same year New York's Letchworth Village officially closed and, like Skillman, now stands as a ghost town.

Standards of the Times

The emphasis in this book has been on a single aspect of "negative" eugenics—forced sterilization of mentally challenged people, and especially how the issue played out in the state of New Jersey—but it would be unfair to overlook countless acts of loving care that were delivered by dedicated nurses, physicians, and administrators at Vineland, Skillman, and similar institutions. Published histories of these facilities usually provide glowing testimonials about the good works once performed there but omit or downplay potentially embarrassing subjects. If many former institutional leaders and political activists were enthusiastic eugenicists, at least we can credit them for genuinely believing that what they espoused was "scientific" and intended for the betterment of mankind.

Henry Goddard's biographer Leila Zenderland suggested that common to many American social scientists during the early twentieth century was simultaneous rejection and indebtedness to the theological ideas of the preceding century:

Like Goddard, many of these writers were children of ministers and missionaries; they too grew up in a world in which intellectual authority was slowly but surely shifting from faith to science. For such persons, knowledge could no longer rest on dogma; it now required scientific proof.

Although eager to embrace the liberating intellectual freedom promised by modern science, Goddard tried to do so without sacrificing all of the values he had acquired from his Quaker upbringing, many of which he still cherished. As a result, much of the social science he produced suggested a deeper process of reconciliation, a process that posed difficult challenges of its own: how to reground social morality in a new foundation of scientific certainty.[67]

Henry Goddard was typical for his time. In her book *Preaching Eugenics,* Christine Rosen explained that although many Protestant, Catholic, and Jewish leaders rejected eugenics, others enthusiastically embraced it—perhaps hoping to remain relevant in secular society by integrating emerging scientific ideas into their own moral frameworks. During the 1920s and 1930s several liberally inclined Protestant and Jewish leaders joined the American Eugenics Society and endorsed eugenics theory from their pulpits. Probably most of these clergymen had little grasp of the fundamentals of science, and their sermons emphasized the positive outcomes that eugenics promised rather than discussing the means that were being proposed to achieve well-meaning goals. As one Protestant minister put it, "Surely the Kingdom can never come in all its fullness among a people descended from the Jukes."[68]   A Reform rabbi in New York linking birth control and eugenics declared, "we can prevent the defectives from bringing forth abundantly and peopling the earth after their own kind."[69]   Others found religion and eugenics to be antithetical, and in 1930 Pope Pius XI issued an unambiguous encyclical about family planning which criticized the eugenics movement for its misplaced priorities:

For there are some who, over solicitous for the cause of eugenics, not only give salutary counsel for more certainly procuring the strength and health of the future child—which, indeed, is not contrary to right reason—but put eugenics before aims of a higher order, and by public authority wish to prevent from marrying all those who, even though naturally fit for marriage, they consider, according to the norms and conjectures of their investigations, would through hereditary transmission, bring forth defective offspring and more, they wish to legislate to deprive these of that natural faculty by medical action despite their unwillingness.... Those who act in this way are at fault in losing sight of the fact that the family is more sacred than the State.[70]

In 1925 the Scopes "monkey trial" enthralled the country; it was the epic battle between creationists and evolutionists—William Jennings Bryan vs. Clarence Darrow. Yet, similar debates continue to roil today. What should be taught in elementary school? What are the moral limits of genetic engineering? What is more important, quality or quantity of life? An international survey of 2,901 geneticists published in 1998 suggested that "eugenics is alive and well." With the exception of China, most geneticists held a pessimistic view of persons with hereditary disabilities and favored individualized genetic counseling after prenatal diagnosis so long as it was not biased by government policy.[71]

More significant than abstract considerations are the outcomes that can emerge when a particular point of view comes to dominate public policy and dictate decision making. The narrative of eugenics, as described here, illustrates how advocacy of forced sterilization as a solution to certain social problems could lead to abuse of individual rights of autonomy. In effect, the strong were allowed and even encouraged to dominate the weak. In the United States when this kind of ideology transformed into state law, more than sixty-five thousand Americans were sterilized against their will—in many cases even without their knowledge. Of course, what happened in Nazi Germany was infinitely worse. I do not mean to suggest that most American eugenicists were complicit in the final outcome of Nazi policy; more likely most of them were naïve or deluded or preferred to deny what the Nazis were capable of, and eventually most of them qualified their public statements.

Coerced sterilization did not entirely disappear after the end of World War II, continuing in this country into the 1970s and beyond. Even today castration still sometimes is used as punishment for criminals—albeit no longer for the purpose of improving genetic stock—and as late as 1996 it was legal to sterilize epileptics in thirteen states. I've been unable to document that any coerced procedures were performed in New Jersey, but perhaps more than in any other state, influential New Jersey leaders such as E. R. Johnstone, Alexander Johnson, Bleeker Van Wagenen, Henry Goddard, Elizabeth Kite, David Weeks, and Marian Olden during the first decades of the last century collaborated with eugenics theorists in performing field work and disseminating eugenics information that validated and ultimately enabled racially based policies to be implemented elsewhere.

In Nazi Germany sterilization begat euthanasia, which, in turn, begat genocide, but such a progression is not inevitable. Indeed, other countries have had their own sterilization experiences with different outcomes. In Sweden over sixty thousand people, mostly women, were sterilized on eugenic grounds between the 1930s and 1976, when the sterilization law was abolished. Initially these were done for those deemed to be racially inferior, mentally retarded, epileptics, or alcoholics— later for social and economic reasons. In India during Indira Ghandi's leadership a forced sterilization program operated for eighteen months during 1976–1977 before being abandoned because of popular backlash, which led to the government's fall. The Chinese policy of one child per family has been strongly encouraged by the government as well as by many members of society as a means of population control. Shorn of its racist origins, surgical sterilization, mostly in the form of vasectomies, has become the world's foremost method of controlling fertility, with more than one million operations performed each year on men and women across the social spectrum— but none of these countries murdered their citizens.

Moral of the Tale

This cautionary tale of Vineland, "The Village of Happiness," and Skillman Village for Epileptics and other institutions like them should remind us that in some respects things were not so different on this side of the Atlantic nearly a century ago than they were in Germany. We should not forget that Germany was a civilized place where people loved their children, went to church, tended their gardens, and listened to Bach and Beethoven—yet the great majority of these "ordinary" people acquiesced with Hitler's policies. To be sure, American scientists didn't participate in selections of tens of thousands of handicapped people for "mercy killing," and, as historian Mark Largent has argued, we should be cautious in demonizing all eugenicists as proto-Nazis or the movement as an aberration in American history, for even today we share many of the same assumptions that once bred such contempt for those deemed to be "socially inadequate."[72]

The modern field of genetics has tried hard to distance itself from its antecedents. Nevertheless, as one historian suggested, "genetics is blemished by the fingerprints of its own history." Some see eugenics practices as applications of Darwinism, but in a strict sense "natural selection" implies that whatever happens, in fact, is natural, and that whoever survives is "fit." In contrast, eugenics theory requires that selection is artificially manipulated according to some judgment about what constitutes fitness. In Nazi Germany the "unfit" were officially designated as "useless eaters" or "lives less worthy." Even today in our own country there are overtones which would value certain categories of people on qualitative grounds. Is the greater good well served by spending limited resources on the terminally ill, the permanently vegetative, the deformed young, or the demented elderly? Who decides and how? In the future these questions are likely to perturb even more as our nation is forced to contend with increasing economic challenges.

Some historians argue that it's unfair to overemphasize the similarities between the American and German eugenicists because this may diminish the seriousness of the atrocities unleashed by Nazi policy. Nevertheless, if we discount common origins we risk losing sight of the fact that we share certain human failings. Drs. Sofair and Kaljdian recently observed:

> Sources of inspiration common to both nations included the belief that scientific management could solve social problems by preventing the propagation of the "unfit"; a willingness to measure individual worth in economic terms to justify strategies to diminish the number, and therefore the cost, of defective populations; the conviction that mental illness posed a serious enough social threat to justify compulsory eugenic sterilization at the cost of the individual right to procreate; and the belief that certain "races" are superior to others.... Both countries established compulsory eugenic sterilization, Germany with totalitarian completeness and the United States according to the decisions of individual states.[73]

Obviously there were significant differences as well. In Germany human and scientific values were subordinated to the priorities of the Nazi regime; utilitarianism supplanted religious and ethical considerations, the medical profession became politicized, there was a calamitous economic crisis, and as a result of all these and more, compulsory sterilization was pursued aggressively. By contrast, the American medical profession was more sensitive to public opinion and willing to question the assumptions and claims of the eugenics movement. Scientific evidence was demanded, and when found to be faulty, led to reassessment and consensus that if eugenic sterilization was to be permitted at all, it should be voluntary and transparent. A democratic process of gradualism, public debate, legal adjudication, and scientific reevaluation eventually brought an end to the madness.

Cold Spring Harbor Laboratory, where Charles Davenport and Harry Laughton spewed racist ideology, transformed into a center of genetics research and eight Nobel Prize winners have served on its faculty. However, the world "eugenics" doesn't appear on the laboratory's web site. Instead, the high-minded mission statement speaks of dedication to molecular biology and curing cancer and other diseases. For nearly forty years Cold Spring Harbor was headed by James B. Watson, who won the Nobel Prize for co-discovering the double helix of DNA. Then in 2003 when interviewed on British television, Watson made a disturbing remark:

If you are really stupid, I would call that a disease. The lower 10% who really have difficulty, even in elementary school, what's the cause of it? A lot of people would like to say— 'Well, poverty, things like that.' It probably isn't. So I'd like to get rid of that, to help the lower 10%.[74]

This rhetoric—the talk of the lower 10 percent and "getting rid of that," is reminiscent of words that were used in the past by Watson's predecessors at Cold Spring Harbor. Evidently James Watson's remarks caused such a furor that he was asked to resign his position. Perhaps Watson was misunderstood; perhaps not. Most people prefer to believe that their actions are well-meaning. So did eugenicists in New Jersey less than a century ago—all respectable people working according to the standards of their day to make the world a better place.

It's easy to dismiss eugenically inspired sterilization as having been based on pseudoscience, but Henry Goddard and his colleagues confirmed many of the public's darkest fears about persons who seemed different. They brought the problems of the feebleminded to

America's attention in a new way which overemphasized the social dangers posed by those labeled as being "unfit" or "morons." If this disturbing tale of the villages teaches nothing else, it should be that good intentions can have unanticipated consequences—sometimes leading to shameful results.

A Bizarre Epilogue

In the preface to this book I described the testimony of the convicted war criminal Dr. Edwin Katzen-Ellenbogen, who worked briefly in New Jersey at Skillman Village. Compared with the celebrated Nuremberg trials at which Nazi leaders were prosecuted, the U.S. Army tribunals that were held at Dachau in 1947 are barely remembered today. These proceedings focused on hundreds of functionaries who were responsible for carrying out orders that had been devised by the leadership. They included guards, officers, and doctors who were not accused of "crimes against humanity" *per se* but were "voluntary enablers." As a former prisoner, at first Dr. Katzen-Ellenbogen served as a witness for the prosecution, but as the facts began to emerge the witness became one of the accused.

Born in the Austro-Hungarian Empire in 1884 into a Jewish family (Katzen-Ellenbogen was the surname of a distinguished line of European rabbis) he was educated in Europe and claimed to have received a medical degree at the University of Leipzig.. In 1905 he immigrated to the United States, married the daughter of a Massachusetts Supreme Court judge, converted to her Catholicism, was naturalized, and worked briefly as a volunteer in New York City hospitals. After about two years there he took a position at the state mental hospital in Danvers, Massachusetts and during this period he sometimes lectured on abnormal psychology at Harvard Medical School. He was a founding member of the American Eugenics

Research Association, and was listed in *American Men of Science*. According to the doctor's testimony at Dachau, in 1911 he became the "scientific director" at Skillman Village where he was "New Jersey's leading expert on epilepsy," and was asked by Governor Wilson to draft a mandatory sterilization law.

The only problem with this narrative is that much of it is bogus! In fact, the doctor's claim to have drafted New Jersey's sterilization law at Governor Wilson's request is entirely implausible. On July 20, 1911, nearly five months *after* the sterilization bill was introduced into the New Jersey legislature, Skillman's Dr. David Weeks wrote the following to his colleague Charles Davenport:

> Dr. Edwin Katzen-Ellenbogen came to the Institution on Monday and made application for the position of Clinical Psychologist. I will be indebted to you if you will give me your opinion of his ability to fill such a position. Anything you know about his personal habits. In brief, anything which you may be able to tell me about the Doctor.

Charles Davenport replied:

> I know nothing about Dr. Katzen-Ellenbogen except such as obtained in a conversation with him for about three or four hours at Cold Spring Harbor a few days ago. He showed me a draft of a paper of his on inheritance in different forms of insanity [which] struck me as being a large work, involving a high degree of analytical ability. He tells me that he has been for some years in the Danvers State Hospital and teaching in the Harvard Medical School.[75]

This correspondence, which is preserved in the Davenport archives of the American Philosophical Society, fails to support Katzen-Ellenbogen's claims either that he was New Jersey's "leading expert on epilepsy" or that he had drafted New Jersey's sterilization law. Indeed, minutes of Skillman's board of trustees indicate that in January of 1911 five leaders from Vineland and Skillman, including Katzen-Ellenbogen's future boss Dr. Weeks, drafted the sterilization law which was introduced to the state legislature several months *before* Katzen-Ellenbogen even had arrived in New Jersey.

There were other factual discrepancies as well. At the Dachau trial Katzen-Ellenbogen testified that he'd been a coeditor of *Epilepsia*, an international medical journal. However, the current editor of *Epilepsia* was unable to verify that Katzen-Ellenbogen ever held such a position.[76] Katzen-Ellenbogen did publish several articles during this period, one of which identified him as "M.D., formerly an Assistant Physician at Danvers State Hospital in Massachusetts and Lecturer in Abnormal Psychology at Harvard (1909-1910)." [77] Another article, which appeared in *Epilepsia* in 1912, listed him as "Dr. Edwin Katzen-Ellenbogen, Director, Psychopathological Laboratory at Skillman."[78] No "M.D." is cited.

This raises the question whether or not Katzen-Ellenbogen actually was a physician. To be sure there is evidence that he participated in "medical studies" in Leipzig and that in 1907 he received a PhD degree there, but a second account of his testimony at the Dachau trials reversed the possible time sequence: "I studied with the father of modern psychology, Wilhelm Wundt. In the course of my studies, I became enormously interested in abnormal and forensic psychology so I took a second study subject, medicine, and graduated first in philosophy and then in medicine from the University of Leipzig." [79] By this account an MD degree would have followed the PhD, placing it *after* 1907, when he already was working in the United States. When I arranged for two researchers in Leipzig to independently check archival records, they were unable to find evidence that Edwin Katzen-Ellenbogen ever received a degree in medicine.

Employment records from Skillman indicated that in August 1911 Katzen-Ellenbogen was hired as a "clinical psychologist" for a one-year probationary period at a salary of $1,000; the next year he was reappointed for $1,800. Skillman's annual report that year listed him as an "administrative assistant and psychopathologist" with AM (master's) and PhD degrees—again, no medical degree is mentioned. Katzen-Ellenbogen left Skillman in December 1912 when Dr. Weeks decided to close the Psychopathology Laboratory. A clue as to why the superintendent let him go can be inferred from several comments he wrote on Katzen-Ellenbogen's personnel record:

"shirked and neglected duties. Disorganizing spirit. Capable of doing first class work but lacked application."[80]

About one year after New Jersey's Supreme Court revoked the state's sterilization law, Dr. Katzen-Ellenbogen set sail for Europe and never returned to this country. His activities over the next two decades were not described in much detail at Dachau, but many years later they were documented by a German doctoral candidate whose dissertation considered the rather esoteric subject of *revocations* of doctoral degrees from the University of Leipzig over a period of five centuries. According to this study, when he returned to Europe Katzen-Ellenbogen developed an unsavory reputation as a swindler, forger, extortionist, bigamist, and drug peddler, and twice was arrested. He preyed upon gullible foreigners and women who advertised in newspapers seeking husbands, using their money for his own real estate investments. Twice authorities in Leipzig were queried about his academic credentials and because of Katzen-Ellenbogen's bad character, the university faculty was asked to revoke his "doctoral" degree.[81]

When the German net tightened for those of Jewish descent, Katzen-Ellenbogen fled to Czechoslovakia, then to Italy, and finally to France. In September 1943 he was arrested by the Gestapo and sent to Buchenwald. While incarcerated there he was hated by fellow prisoners because it was clear that he was collaborating with the Germans. Most prisoners worked and starved into skeletons, but he ate well and received special privileges. Reputedly he was responsible for sending many to their deaths; he was even accused of directly murdering prisoners with injections of phenol. Responding to this last allegation at his trial, the doctor nonchalantly replied that it could not be proved. In this he was correct because there were none still alive to give personal testimony.

Among Katzen-Ellenbogen's responsibilities at Buchenwald was to decide who entered the camp hospital. He was accused of striking prisoners and accepting bribes of cigarettes or food for favored treatment. Sometimes he falsified diagnoses, and he even coached some prisoners about how to fake symptoms. As described by Edwin Black: "On the witness stand Katzen-Ellenbogen was asked if someone could be trained to feign symptoms. In reply he boasted, 'To throw a fit? With training, he could do it. I myself, for instance, could give a wonderful performance in that respect.'" In another exchange with the prosecutor, Katzen-Ellenbogen described how during experiments he'd performed at Harvard, someone might make a statement and then several weeks later say something entirely different. Tellingly, he added, "I am not above that myself."

This recurring theme of faking symptoms or confabulating recalls an article that Katzen-Ellenbogen published in 1911 in which he described a cat and mouse game he played in order to break down the alibi of a criminal who was pleading innocence on the basis of insanity, until the man admitted that he was fabricating his story. Perhaps a lifelong tendency to prevaricate helps to explain Katzen-Ellenbogen's behavior at the Dachau trial, during which he gave the impression of being an expert in the nuances of both German and American law. During the trial many found Dr. Katzen-Ellenbogen to be incomprehensible, alternatively a gifted psychiatrist and a murderous physician, sometimes capable of exhibiting compassion toward those he saw as superior, and yet capable of great cruelty toward those he considered unfit. He seemed to be a man without a conscience, indifferent to the well-being of others. Unremorseful, deceitful, yet outwardly appearing to be normal—the psychopathologist exhibited the classic symptoms of being a psychopath.

The very same year that Edwin Black published his book about the American eugenics movement, another investigative reporter, Joshua Greene, published a biography of William Denson, the zealous young lawyer who served as the army's chief prosecutor at Dachau. According to Greene, at the end of the proceedings in the case of Dr. Katzen-Ellenbogen on August 12, 1947, the military tribunal concluded: "It is clear that the accused, although an inmate, cooperated with the SS personnel managing the camp and participated in the common design." In his final statement, playing for effect, the defendant declared:

I am not afraid of death, but I am afraid of life with Cain's stigma on my forehead. I was described here as an SS helper, as a Gestapo helper. Therefore judges, I ask you for one grace. Apply to me the highest penalty, which is in your hands.[82]

The next day Edwin Katzen-Ellenbogen was sentenced to life imprisonment. Afterward, Prosecutor Denson asked members of the tribunal to explain why the doctor's life had been spared? They replied, "He wanted to be hanged and we did not want to accede to his wishes." Denson fumed, "That old goat didn't want to be hanged any more than you or I do. He used his knowledge of psychology to get you to give him a life sentence." But the "old goat" wasn't finished. In March 1950, writing from prison to William Denson, who by then was an attorney for the Atomic Energy Commission and based in Washington, DC, his tone was ingratiating, even collegial:

> Being 68 years old and lying for weeks in bed with critical heart failure, I have lots of leisure to think matters over. Retrospectively I ponder over the Buchenwald trial in which we were adversaries.... You stole the show. I often objectively admired you and having had a vast experience as court expert with District Attorneys I must hand it to you that you were the ablest one. I much enjoyed our duel while I was on the witness stand and you must admit that I scored many points over you. I think we both enjoyed it. But you had a free show while I was in danger to lose my liberty. [83]

Dr. Katzen-Ellenbogen went on to justify his past behavior, apparently in hope that prosecutor Denson would support his request for clemency, as had been granted to other war criminals—but the former prosecutor was not impressed. He considered Katzen-Ellenbogen to be more culpable than the others, most of whom were uneducated; he was a villain who always was aware of what he was doing. However, Katzen-Ellenbogen's appeals did have some effect, for his sentence was reduced, first to fifteen and later to twelve years, because of a heart condition. Then, shortly after sending his letter to Denson, Edwin Katzen-Ellenbogen died in prison of his ailments. His posturing on the witness stand at Dachau may have represented the fabrications of a desperate man, but the tragedy of this one flawed individual pales in comparison to the effect that his fictitious actions might have had on helpless victims in the asylums of New Jersey or to what actually did occur three decades later at Buchenwald.

Dr. Katzen-Ellenbogen's tenure at Skillman lasted for little more than one year, and evidently his imprint in New Jersey was insignificant. But in retrospect his story underscores the danger that can ensue when misguided science transforms into social policy. It also illustrates how in the hands of amoral individuals eugenics ideology could lead to genocide. Concerning eugenics, perhaps Edwin Katzen-Ellenbogen inadvertently said it best. The first paragraph of a paper which he published in 1911 began with these words:

> It is a dangerous enterprise to prematurely apply theoretical findings of any science to practical use, as the frequent failures which result there from not only discourage the workers, but also cast discredit upon the work itself.[84]

Dr. Katzen-Ellenbogen was referring to the then relatively new field of experimental psychology, but what could be a more appropriate epitaph for the eugenics movement itself?

Acknowledgements and Sources

As explained in the preface, my interest in this subject was prompted by reading Edwin Black's book about American eugenics, *War Against The Weak*. A somewhat different perspective on the Dachau trials and Dr. Katzen-Ellenbogen's testimony appears in Joshua Greene's *Justice at Dachau*. Many people helped me to track the veracity of Katzen-Ellenbogen's narrative, including Simon Shorvon, the current editor of the medical journal *Epilepsia*. That one-hundred-year-old publication's Web site also provided many useful articles from early issues. Other sources of primary information concerning Katzen-Ellenbogen's years in New Jersey were found in the archives of the American Philosophical Society, the Academy of Medicine of New York, and the New Jersey State Archives. David F. Weeks, the grandson of Skillman's Dr. David F. Weeks, provided biographical information about his family. Robert Vietrogoski of the G. F. Smith Library of the Health Sciences, UMDNJ-Special Collections, and the Medical History Society of New Jersey was of great help, especially in locating old photographs of Vineland and Skillman. Numerous individuals at other libraries, especially at my local River Vale Public Library, were of unfailing assistance. I apologize for not citing everyone who provided encouragement and suggestions, but I do want to acknowledge three individuals in Germany who traced and translated documents pertaining to Katzen-Ellenbogen's academic record in Leipzig as well as about the early history of the asylum at Bethel: Andrea Lorch, Kerstin Stockheck and Albrecht Seidel.

Details about the history of Skillman Village can be found in Walter Baker's *A History of the New Jersey State Village for Epileptics* (Van Harlingen Historical Society Publications, 2005), Charles Jubenville's *A History of the New Jersey State Village for Epileptics at Skillman* (University Microfilms International, 1957) and Michael Mendelson and Helen Burlingham's *A History of the New Jersey Neuro-Psychiatric Institute* (Van Harlingen Historical Society, 1972). Information about the early days of the Vineland Training School is available in Joseph Byers's, *The Village of Happiness. The Story of the Training School,* Michael Wehmeyer and J.D.Smith's *Leaving the Garden: Reconsidering Henry Herbert Goddard's Exodus From The Vineland Training School (Mental Retardation 2006*: 44: 150-155) and Pearl Buck's *The Child Who Never Grew.* Additional source material about Dr. Goddard and other early eugenicists was found in the Rockland County Historical Society's Letchfield Village archives.

Bibliography

Aziz, Phillipe. *Doctors of Death. Volume Four. The Bethel Rescue Mission.* Geneva: Fermi Publishers, 1976.

Baron, Jeremy. *The Anglo-American Biomedical Antecedents of Nazi Crimes.* New York: Edward Mellon Press, 2007.

Black, Edwin. *War Against the Weak: Eugenics and America's Campaign to Create a Master Race.* New York: Four Walls Eight Windows, 2003.

Brigham, Carl C. *A Study of American Intelligence.* Princeton, NJ: Princeton University Press, 1923.

Bruinius, Harry. *Better for All the World.* New York: Alfred A. Knopf, 2006.

Burleigh, Michael. *Death and Deliverance: 'Euthanasia' in Germany 1900–1945.* Cambridge: Cambridge University Press, 1994.

Davenport, Charles. *Heredity In Relation To Eugenics.* New York: Henry Holt & Co., 1911.

Dowbiggen, Ian. *The Sterilization Movement and Global Fertility in the 20th Century.* Oxford: Oxford University Press, 2008.

Dugdale, Richard. *The Jukes. A Study in Crime, Pauperism, Disease and Heredity.* New York: Putnam, 1910.

Friedlander, Henry. *The Origins of Nazi Genocide.* Chapel Hill, NC: North Carolina University Press, 1995.

Friedlander, Saul. *Nazi Germany and the Jews. Volume I. The Years of Persecution, 1933–1939.* New York: HarperCollins Publishers, 1997.

Friedman, David M. *The Immortalists* (Alexis Carrel). New York: HarperCollins Publishers, 2007.

Galton, Francis. *Hereditary Genius: An Inquiry Into Its Laws and Consequences.* London: Macmillan & Co.,1892.

Gollaher, David. *Voice For The Mad. The Life of Dorothea Dix.* New York: The Free Press, 1995.

Gould, Stephen Jay. *The Mismeasure of Man.* New York: W. W. Norton & Company, 1981.

Grant, Madison. *The Passing of the Great Race.* New York: Charles Scribner's Sons, 1916.

Greene, Joshua. *Justice at Dachau.* New York: Broadway Books, 2003.

Grob, Gerald. *The Mad Among Us: A History of the Care of America's Mentally Ill.* New York: The Free Press, 1994.

Gugliotta, Angela. *Dr. Sharp with His Little Knife: Therapeutic and Punitive Origins of Eugenic Va-sectomy—Indiana, 1892-1921.* New York: Oxford University Press, 1998.

Kuhl, Stefan. *The Nazi Connection: Eugenics, American Racism and German National Socialism.* New York: Oxford University Press, 1994.

Largent, Mark. *Breeding Contempt: The History of Coerced Sterilization in the United States.* New Brunswick: Rutgers University Press, 2008

Leiby, James. *Charity and Correction in New Jersey: A History of State Welfare Institutions.* New Brunswick: Rutgers University Press, 1967.

Lifton, Robert Jay. *The Nazi Doctor: Medical Killing and the Psychology of Genocide.* New York: Basic Books, 1986.

Lombroso, Paul. *Three Generations, No Imbeciles.* Baltimore: The Johns Hopkins University Press, 2008.

Proctor, Robert. *Racial Hygiene: Medicine under the Nazis.* Cambridge, MA: Harvard University Press, 1988.

Reilly, Phillip. *The Surgical Solution: A History of Involuntary Sterilization in the United States.* Baltimore: Johns Hopkins University Press, 1991.

Rosen, Christine. *Preaching Eugenics: Religious Leaders and the American Eugenics Movement.* New York: Palgrave Macmillan, 2004.

Sanger, Margaret. *Woman and the New Race.* New York: Brentano's, 1920.

Scull, Andrew. *Madhouse: A Tragic Tale of Megalomania and Modern Medicine* (Henry Cotton). New Haven: Yale University Press, 2007.

Spiro, Jonathan. *Defending the Master Race. Conservation, Eugenics, and the Legacy of Madison Grant.* Burlington: University of Vermont Press, 2009.

Trent, James W. *Inventing the Feeble Mind.* Berkeley: University of California Press, 1994.

Weikart, Richard. *From Darwin To Hitler.* New York: Palgrave Macmillan, 2004.

Zenderland, Leila. *Measuring Minds.* Cambridge: Cambridge University Press, 1998.

Notes

(for details see above.)

1. Black, *War Against the Weak*.

2. Black, *War Against the Weak*, 125–27.

3. Black, *War Against the Weak*, 322.

4. Grob, *The Mad Among Us*, 1.

5. Leiby, 49–63.

6. J. F. Munson, "Public Care for the Epileptic," *Epilepsia* 1910: 36–43.

7. Scull, *Madhouse*, 66

8. Scull, *Madhouse*, 69.

9. Galton, *Hereditary Genius*, 1.

10. Bruinius, *Better for All the World*, (Sanger) 131–133; (Shaw) 152; (Roosevelt) 191.

11. Davenport, *Heredity in Relation to Eugenics*, 1.

12 Joseph Byers, *The Village of Happiness*, 41.

13. New Jersey Training School For Feeble-Minded Girls and Boys, 20th Annual Report, 1908, 39.

14. Classics in the History of Psychology, *The Kallikak Family*, http://psychclassics.yorku.ca/Goddard/chap3.htm

15. Classics in the History of Psychology, *The Kallikak Family*, http://psychclassics.yorku.ca/Goddard/chap3.htm

16. Classics in the History of Psychology, *The Kallikak Family*, http://psychclassics.yorku.ca/Goddard/preface.htm

17. Munson, "Public Care for the Epileptic," 36–43.

18. David F. Weeks, "What New Jersey Is Doing For the Epileptic," *Archives Pediatrics*, 29 (1912): 303–11.

19. Gugliotta, *Dr. Sharp with His Little Knife*, 371–406.

20. Bruinius, *Better for All the World*, 208.

21. *Life at Letchworth Village*, The 40th Annual Report of the Board of Visitors for the Fiscal Year ended March 31, 1948, State of New York, Department of Mental Hygiene, 136.

22. Supreme Court of NJ, *Smith v. Board of Examiners*. 85 N.J.L. 46; 88A. 963; 1913.

23. Edwin Johnstone, *Epilepsia* 3 (1911): 98.

24. W. T. Shanahan, "A Plea for Moderate Conservatism in the Care and Treatment of Epileptics." *Epilepsia* 4 (1912): 122.

25. Bruinius, *Better for All the World*, 173.

26. H. M. Carey, "Compulsory Segregation and Sterilization of the Feeble-minded and Epileptic," *Epilepsia* 3 (1911): 86.

27 Johnstone, *Epilepsia* 3 (1911): 96–99.

28. Supreme Court of NJ, *Smith v. Board of Examiners*, 85 N.J.L. 46; 88A. 963; 1913.

29. Harry Laughlin, Eugenics Record Office, *Bulletin 10B*, (1914): 59–61.

30. "Sterilization of the Mentally Defective in State Institutions," Case Note, *Yale Law Journal* 1918; 28:189.

31. Supreme Court of NJ, *Smith v. Board of Examiners*, 85 N.J.L. 46; 88A. 963; 1913.

32. Robert McCarter, *Memories of a Half Century at the New Jersey Bar*, New Jersey State Bar Association, 1937, 43–47.

33. Trent. *Inventing The Feeble Mind*, 173–77.

34. William C. Graves. "American Association for the Study of Epilepsy. President's Address," *Epilepsia* (1915): 248–53.

35. 14th Annual Report, Board of Managers of Letchworth Village, State of New York (1923): 20–21.

36. Bruinius, *Better for All the World*, 60.

37. Bruinius, *Better for All the World*, 71–72.

38 Bruinius, *Better for All the World*, 324.

39. Baron, *The Anglo-American Biomedical Antecedents of Nazi Crimes*, 93.

40 Zenderland, *Measuring Minds*, 293.

41. Dowbiggin, *The Sterilization Movement*, 38.

42. Dowbiggin, *The Sterilization Movement*, 37.

43. Kuhl, *The Nazi Connection*, 58–59.

44. Dowbiggin, *The Sterilization Movement*, 40.

45. Philip Reilly, *Genetics, Law and Social Policy*, Harvard University Press, 1977, 124.

46. David Friedman, *The Immortalists*, Harper Collins, 2007, 88.

47. A. Sofair and L. Kaldjian, L. "Eugenic sterilization and a qualified Nazi analogy: The United States and Germany, 1930-1945," *Annals Intern Med* 132 (2000): 312–19.

48. Black, *War Against the Weak*, 313.

49. Kuhl, *The Nazi Connection*, 87.

50. Proctor, *Racial Hygiene*, 97.

51. Burleigh, *Death and Deliverance*, 11.

52. Proctor, *Racial Hygiene*, 112–14.

53. Friedlander, *The Origins of Nazi Genocide*, 290.

54. Rael Strauss, "Nazi Euthanasia of the Mentally Ill at Hadamar," *Am J Psychiatry* 163 (2006): 27.

55. Friedlander, *The Origins of Nazi Genocide*, 115.

56. Black, *War Against the Weak*, 415–16.

57. New Jersey State Archives, Skillman Village, Board of Managers Minutes, November 1912.

58. Burleigh, *Death and Deliverance*, 5.

59. Burleigh, *Death and Deliverance*, 117.

60. Aziz, *Doctors of Death*, 223.

61. Lifton. *The Nazi Doctors*, 122.

62. Dorothea Buck, "70 Years of Coercion in German Psychiatric Institutions, Experienced and Witnessed," Speech delivered June 7, 2007, Dresden, Germany. http://www.bpe-online.de/1/buck-wpa-2007-e.pdf

63. Pearl S. Buck, *The Child Who Never Grew*, Woodbine House, Inc., 1992.

64. *Life at Letchworth Village*, The 40th Annual Report of the Board of Visitors For the Fiscal Year Ended March 31, 1948, State of New York, Department of Mental Hygiene, 136.

65. Trent, *Inventing the Feeble Mind*, 227.

66. Supreme Court of New Jersey, *In the Matter of Grady*, 426 N.E. 2d 467 (1981).

67. Zenderland, *Measuring Minds*, 363.

68. Rosen, *Preaching Eugenics*, 122.

69. Rosen, *Preaching Eugenics*, 156.

70. Rosen, *Preaching Eugenics*, 158–59.

71. Wertz DC, Fletcher JC, et al, "Has patient autonomy gone too far? Geneticists' views in 36 Nations," *Am J Bioeth.* 2002; 2: W21.

72 Largent, *Breeding Contempt*, 90.

73. Sofair and Kaldjian, 315—16.

74. Black, *War Against the Weak*, 442–43.

75. Correspondence between Charles Davenport and David F. Weeks, American Philosophical Society Library, Charles B. Davenport Papers, Series II; BD 27.

76. Personal communication, Prof. Simon Shorvon, London, June 20, 2008.

77. Edwin Katzen-Ellenbogen, "The Detection of a Case of Simulation of Insanity By Means of Association Tests," *Journal of Abnormal Psychology* 6 (1911): 19.

78. Edwin Katzen-Ellenbogen, "The Mental Efficiency in Epileptics," *Epilepsia* 3 (1912): 504.

79. Greene, *Justice at Dachau*, 295–315.

80. New Jersey State Archives, Skillman Village, Personnel Register, Box 41.

81. Jens Blecher, *Vom Promotionsprivileg zum Promotionsrecht.* (doctoral dissertation) Halle-Wittenberg: Martin Luther University, 1965, 242–47.

82. Greene, *Justice at Dachau*, 314–15.

83 Greene, *Justice at Dachau*, 344–45.

84. Edwin Katzen-Ellenbogen, "The Detection of a Case of Simulation of

Insanity By Means of Association Tests," *Journal of Abnormal Psychology* 6 (1911): 19.

Printed in the United States
149881LV00004B/4/P

9 781440 142611